Messages that Move

How to give Bible talks that challenge and inspire

Tim Hawkins

Messages that move:
How to give Bible talks that challenge and inspire
© Tim Hawkins 2013

ISBN: 9781908762375

Published by The Good Book Company
Blenheim House, 1 Blenheim Road, Epsom, Surrey KT19 9AP, UK
Tel: 0333 123 0880; **International:** +44 (0) 208 942 0880
Email: admin@thegoodbook.co.uk

The Good Book Company (USA)
170 W. Main St, Purcellville VA, 20132
Tel: 866 244 2165; International: +1 866 244 2165
Email: sales@thegoodbook.com

Websites:
UK: www.thegoodbook.co.uk
North America: www.thegoodbook.com
Australia: www.thegoodbook.com.au
New Zealand: www.thegoodbook.co.nz

Published in Australia as *Preach like a Train Driver.*

Design: André Parker
Printed and bound by CPI Group (UK) Ltd, Croydon, CR0 4YY

Contents

This book is dedicated to all the faithful
Bible teachers, youth leaders, pastors and preachers
who have taught me so much
from God's precious word.

What this book is – *and what it is not*

Whoen I studied at theological college, I had a very thorough education on how to understand the Bible and discern God's word. We threw around words like "exegesis", "hermeneutics" and "homiletics". It was at theological college that I learned to love God's word, and to plumb its depths so that I knew God richly and intimately.

But no-one taught me *how* to preach God's word **effectively**. And since leaving theological college, I have sat under the teaching of many faithful ministers who loved and knew God's word deeply. And yet many of them struggled to communicate this effectively to their congregations – and to the emerging generation. They were great at being **faithful**, but not so great at being **effective**.

In recent years, I have been running preaching classes for the interns at our church. But every month, I noticed that some members of our pastoral staff – who had been preachers for years – started slipping in at the back and furiously scribbling notes. Despite their expertise and experience as Bible teachers, they wanted to learn more about how to engage their listeners and apply great biblical truths to their hearts.

What this book is not

Understanding God's word correctly is absolutely central and fundamental for any Bible teacher. You cannot be effective in your Bible teaching unless you are first faithful in your Bible understanding. But this book is not meant to be *"The Complete Book of Preaching"*. Nor is it primarily designed to enable you to discover the meaning of God's word in detail (what the theologians call *exegesis*). My main focus is not to help you with your Bible interpretation. There are already plenty of fine publications to assist you with this.

What this book is

Instead, this book is primarily concerned with how you *teach* God's word effectively. How do you engage your listeners right at the start? How do you take them on a worthwhile journey? How do you help your audience to arrive at the biblical destination that God has revealed in His word? In short, how do you preach like a train driver?

If you are a Bible teacher – a youth leader; a beginner at giving Bible talks; or a seasoned preacher – let's learn together how we can be *both* **faithful** *and* **effective** as we bring God's life-giving word to our world.

Tim Hawkins

Chapter 1

Every great message takes people on a journey

"Preach like a train driver?"
"YES! Preach like a train driver!"

I f you ever need to catch a train, then you know we all need train drivers. We place our lives in their hands every time we travel. They are hard-working, and no doubt honourable men and women. But if you've ever listened to a Public Address announcement on a train – you might well be thinking that public speaking is not exactly their strong point!

But a train driver might be more of a model for preaching than you imagine. In its simplest terms, a train driver's job is this: to *take their passengers to the right destination.* That's what you depend on them to do. That is their strong point!

For a train driver to take their passengers successfully to the correct destination, they need to understand and practise three key concepts:

1. They need to understand their destination
* *Where precisely am I taking these passengers?*
* *How do I make sure we get there – promptly and safely?*

2. They need to understand their journey

- *Do I have the right train to get us there?*
- *Am I on the right track to make it?*
- *Are there stations I need to visit along the way?*
- *Am I skilful enough as a driver to get us there?*

3. They need to understand their passengers

- *Where do I pick up my passengers from?*
- *How do I get the passengers on-board my train?*
- *How do I stop the passengers getting off before the journey is completed?*

It's exactly the same for the preacher.

1. You need to understand your destination

- *Where precisely am I taking my listeners?*
- *What is the point of my message? What will make this journey worthwhile?*

2. You need to understand your journey

- *What biblical information will help us get there?*
- *What sub-points do I need to establish to help us to arrive?*
- *Can I see where this single journey fits into God's overall journey for His people?*
- *How do I help people to keep moving to the same destination?*

3. You need to understand your passengers

- *Where do I pick up my listeners from?*
- *What are they already thinking about this topic before I begin?*
- *How do I get my listeners on-board my train?*
- *How do I stop them getting off before the journey is completed?*

Great Bible talks will take their listeners to a destination worth going to. Of all the brilliant messages I have heard over all these years, the ones that really impacted me were the ones that **took me to a destination where I needed to go**. Maybe before the message I didn't realise that I needed to go to that destination, but the speaker knew what station to call at to collect me; they knew how to engage me so I wanted to travel on their train; they stopped me getting off before my journey was completed; and because they faithfully took me to a godly destination, my life was changed for ever.

Does this ring true for you? Have you ever heard any great sermons? Life-changing messages that marked a significant spiritual step for you? Think about these Bible talks for a moment. **These are the messages that took you where God wanted you to go.** A great message always has a great destination!

On the other hand, you've probably heard enough messages that took you **absolutely nowhere**. Maybe the preacher had all the right information; maybe they had a sound theology; maybe they knew their Bible well; maybe they told really funny stories ... **but they took you nowhere!** There was no destination; there was no journey; no-one's life got changed. You never want to proclaim a message like that!

The most significant thing I have ever learned in preaching is that no matter what I am saying, my aim is to take my listeners to a destination. This revolutionised my thinking!

I used to think of a sermon merely as an *informational* exercise – that is, my job as a preacher was to dispense information.

At other times I saw that preaching was an *inspirational* exercise – to motivate people to listen and believe.

Sometimes I thought that Bible talks were just a *theological* exercise – to get people to believe the right things, and they'd start living the right way.

There were times when I thought that preaching was primarily a *pastoral* exercise – you know, give support and comfort to all those Christians who are living in stressful and difficult times.

I have also believed that preaching was mainly a *confrontational* exercise – where I could identify the sins of the congregation – thrust the double-edge sword of God's word into those gaping wounds – then give the knife a quarter twist to the right to increase the pain – so that the outcome would be profound repentance.

And indeed I have often seen preaching as being primarily an *evangelistic* exercise – its main aim being to bring the unbeliever to the cross of Jesus to start a new life of hope and glory.

All these things matter. Yes, you do need to have right information in what you teach. Your message should certainly be inspirational – and pastoral – and confrontational. Of course your theology matters – otherwise you will end up proclaiming doctrines that God never believed in! And every chance I get, I love to be evangelistic!

All these are important, but if I don't take my listeners to a destination that is worth going to, then I have wasted their time. The essence of any journey is that you take people to a worthwhile destination.

Why do people go on a journey? Any journey? OK, sometimes they are train buffs and just want to ride a grand old steam engine. But most of the time, it's the **destination** that compels people to take a journey. They want to go to work; they want to see the wonders of the world; they want to be reunited with their long lost friend; they want to witness their favourite team play; or they simply want to get home.

That's why people travel. Not because of the train, the bus, the boat or the plane. It's the **destination** that motivates them for the journey. As motivational speaker Lisa Sasevich says:

> *"People are buying the destination –*
> *not the plane"*

Many Bible teachers like to polish up their train. You know, great stories, video clips, funny moments, dynamic PowerPoints, emotional cliff-hangers. You can practise and hone your craft until it reaches the heights of dizzy excellence (which might not be a bad idea!). But if you preach like a train driver, people are listening not because your train means something to them – they are listening because your destination is somewhere they desperately want to go. The essence of being a good train driver is that you can persuade people that your train is worth getting on, and then take them convincingly to a God-given destination which will be life-changing.

But not every journey leads to a worthwhile destination. Read on!

Chapter 2

Every great message takes people to a destination

Not every Bible talk makes it to the destination. Some fall far short. There are some train trips that do not take people anywhere, because something else jumps in and stops the journey.

Let's check out four messages – four journeys – that never take anyone anywhere.

1. The carnival ride
The journey with no destination

There are, of course, journeys that deliberately have no destination. They take people nowhere. They deliver you back exactly where you started. These are called carnival rides. People willingly pay their money, line up for hours, and take the thrill ride of their life. Lots of fun. Well worth doing.

I love roller coasters. One of my dreams is to do a tour of the theme parks of the USA. I love every part of the journey: the steep climbs, the stomach-lifting drops, the breakneck speed, the disorienting loops. So much fun! And if you're not careful, so much upset in your stomach! I love having a good time!

But the purpose of preaching is not just to give people a good time. Our purpose is to take them to a God-given destination. Otherwise we will fall into the trap that the Bible warns us about:

> For the time will come when people will not put up with sound doctrine. Instead, to suit their own desires, they will gather round them a great number of teachers to say what their itching ears want to hear. **2 Timothy 4:3**

If entertainment is our goal as Bible teachers, then our listeners will end up in the same dire situation as the residents and visitors in ancient Athens:

> All the Athenians and the foreigners who lived there spent their time doing nothing but talking about and listening to the latest ideas. **Acts 17:21**

If we just want to give people a good time, let's stop calling ourselves preachers and start calling ourselves comedians or entertainers. Nothing wrong with comedians and entertainers, but preachers are called to achieve far more than to stimulate people's senses for a moment. We are called to bring people face to face with God, and for them to be challenged and changed by meeting with him.

> Preach the word; be prepared in season and out of season; correct, rebuke and encourage with great patience and careful instruction. **2 Timothy 4:2**

If you give your Bible talk – and you don't take us to a worthwhile destination – then you're just taking us all for a ride.

2. The broken-down train
The journey that never starts
There are other journeys that never even leave their starting point.

Have you ever been on one of those journeys? You *thought* you'd get to your destination; you *hoped* you'd get to your destination, you *prayed* that you'd get to your destination – but something went wrong. The plane stayed on the runway. The train ground to a halt because of a signal failure. The bus driver took a wrong turn. You got a puncture. Your car died and had to be towed away. It happens to all of us. It is so *frustrating* when you never reach your destination!

My daughter and I were all signed up for the big trip to Israel. The adventure of a lifetime! The tickets were all booked and paid for, and we dutifully showed up at London's Heathrow Airport and joined the queue for our airline, BMI, which seemed to stretch somewhere into the next postcode area. An hour or so later, we finally arrived at the cheery check-in girl who announced in a sort of concerned but chirpy voice: *"I'm sorry, I can't allocate you a seat. The flight is overbooked and you've been bumped."*

This was a journey where we were going nowhere. We had been promised a destination. We were committed to travelling to that destination. We were eagerly looking forward to that destination. But we weren't going to get there. Not on BMI. Not that day.

Have you ever had to listen to a talk like that? A message where the destination was announced, but nobody ever arrived there? Maybe the preacher never made it either! Maybe the speaker knew their Bible well; maybe they had all the right information; but whatever else they achieved in their message, nobody arrived at any destination that day. Not with that preacher. Not with that message.

3. The de-railed train
The preacher who gets distracted from the destination

My wife and I once took our two teenage kids on the once-in-a-lifetime-let's-take-the-kids-to-Disneyland trip. After we had safely arrived in Anaheim, we settled down for a week in one of those squillion motels that sit across the road from Disneyland, where we were entirely surrounded by a myriad of other intrepid tourists. Eventually, when we had Disneylanded ourselves out, we realised that we had a spare day with nothing to do.

"Let's go to Mexico!" someone said.

Seemed like a great idea. We had a hire-car at our disposal; it was only a few hours drive away. What could be simpler? A few hours drive, a wonderful day in Tijuana, sample the Mexican hospitality, devour the Mexican food, grab ourselves some souvenir sombreros. This trip had "great destination" written all over it.

We set off around 9am. After we had been driving for around an hour, we knew we had left the city limits well behind. We were travelling on the highway through some very sparsely populated land, and as we turned the corner, there, rising from out of the desert, like a Shangri-La in the wilderness, was this gi-normous factory-outlet centre. Right there in the middle of nowhere was one of the biggest retail centres we had ever seen!

"Honey, look!" exclaimed my wife. *"Factory Outlets! Let's stop and shop for a while."* I looked at my watch – the day was fairly tightly timetabled – and I replied with a sigh in my voice: *"We don't have time to go shopping today. We're going to Mexico!"*

Noticing the scowl on my wife's face, I turned to my 16-year-old daughter for support. *"Carly – we're going to Mexico, right?"*

"But dad – it's a factory outlet!"

I knew I could count on my 13-year-old son. *"Hey Josh – it'll be really cool to go to Mexico… right?"* He looked at me in that wistful way that only 13 year old boys can master.

"Dad, it's factory outlets – and they've got Nike and Puma and Adidas and…"

I could sense that a chant of *"Factory outlets, factory outlets…"* was about to erupt from the entire family. So with a cursory glance of my watch, I finally gave in: *"OK – half an hour's shopping, and then we're going to Mexico!"*

Six hours later, we were still at the factory-outlet centre. At four in the afternoon, I reluctantly conceded – *"We've stayed here too long. We'll never make it to Mexico today"*. I was right on both counts. We had – so we didn't. We made it home with lots of goodies – lots of new clothes, new shoes, yummy food and futuristic electronic gizmos. But on our journey that had started so well – we were terminally detoured. We never made it to our destination. *Ever.*

You've heard Bible talks like that, right? The preacher starts out towards a great destination – makes enormous headway – and then gets distracted by some side issue – some minor point – some theological idea that fascinates their senses with loads of scriptural temptations – but it is a side-track, a detour, and nobody ever arrives at the magnificent destination that God had clearly laid out in Scripture.

If you're preaching like a train driver, don't get derailed and detoured along the way, no matter how fascinating you find any of the stations or branch lines.

4. The empty train
The preacher who neglects to pick up their passengers
Of course, sometimes the Bible teacher has a grand old journey. Pulls out of the station full-steam ahead; drives their shiny new train at breakneck speed; understands the track, knows the signals, checks the stations… indeed does everything imaginable to arrive at the destination with a cheery grin on their face. Safely and promptly. A smooth journey.

Only problem is… **nobody got on their train.**

They never picked up their passengers! They never persuaded anyone to join them for the journey. As they charged out of their departure point with the engine revving, every one of their passengers remained firmly on the platform. They could see no reason to get on that particular train. They never bought into the destination and they never saw any reason to leave the comfort of the departure lounge for the uncertainty of a train journey. As the eager preacher pulled out of the station with eyes only for the destination, every one of their potential passengers remained firmly on the platform waving *"Bye, bye preacher – have a nice journey – all by yourself!"*

Let me announce clearly to you the destination of this book: *that every time you preach God's word, you take your listeners on a journey to a life-changing destination that God has revealed in his word.* That's where I want to head with you. That's what I want to show you step by step. If you're prepared to travel with me on this journey, I believe that God will equip you to be far more impactful in your Bible teaching than you would otherwise be.

Imagine what it would be like if every message from every preacher genuinely took their listeners to a God-glorifying destination? Imagine what it would be like for people to be no longer bored by preaching, but *energised* by it – challenged to change their ways and excited to reach the destination that God had planned. And imagine if every destination was not just "more information" or "more understanding" or "I got all my main points to spell A-W-E-S-O-M-E" – but that the destination always meant "life-change"!

> *Are you game to venture on this journey with me?*
> *Come on, let's go!*

Chapter 3

The only real destination is transformation

The first trip that my wife and I took after we were married was a driving trip around Tasmania. This is a beautiful part of the world, and well worth visiting. We were driving a small campervan (RV), so we more or less made up the itinerary as we went. We would look ahead – find somewhere interesting on the map – and book into a caravan park for the night.

We decided to visit one of the smaller communities on the north coast. I'm not quite sure why. It was a little bit of a detour from where we were heading – but it looked interesting on the map. And there was a reasonably priced caravan park right in the middle of town.

It was quite late by the time we arrived; the sun was setting and darkness was fast approaching. We searched the grey horizon for any sign of our caravan park that we had booked. We were tired – and ready to rest after a full day's driving.

Finally, we saw a battered sign announcing our destination. At last, rest was within our grasp! It looked kind of different as we drove in, but it was the only caravan park in town – so we dutifully paid our money and headed to our appointed spot. Actually – we could have picked **any** spot at all – there were no other visitors of any description staying the night. Then we noticed there were no trees – no lawns – no gardens. The whole park was a sea of bitumen surrounded by a barbed-wire fence. As darkness fell, a strong cold wind swept up and raced across this open sea of black tar. It was cold, wet, drab and miserable. We cooked our dinner huddled around our little gas stove and retreated to our campervan to survive the ordeal.

This tiny community may well have been the nicest town on earth, but that night we learned something about their caravan park. **It was not designed for tourists!** The park was there to cater for the workers who would travel down to work on a hydro-electric scheme. It was a basic, bare-minimum park for those who **had** to be there anyway. For us, it was a huge disappointment. We couldn't wait to leave the next morning. It was a destination that was not worth going to.

If you're going to take your listeners to a destination, **you need to make sure that the destination is worth going to!** And can I suggest right now that there is only one destination worth taking people to? It's a destination called *"Change-ville"*. It is the **destination of gospel transformation.** The point of your sermon – the point of your message – is that people will change something about their life. I want to suggest to you that if your destination does not focus on life change, then the journey was not worth the effort.

For your destination to be worthwhile and meaningful for your audience, something in them has to change. Something in their lives needs to be challenged to be different. When you think you have worked out the destination for your journey, ask these questions about your audience:

- *How will they think differently?*
- *How will they feel differently?*
- *How will they act differently?*

A destination that can answer these three key questions is a destination that is well worth going to.

I have heard many Bible talks that have taken people to a destination, but that destination fell far short of challenging people to change their lives – or change anything, for that matter.

There are three competing models when it comes to destinations in a Bible talk:

1. "I know more"
The destination of information

Part of your journey will be to increase people's knowledge and understanding about a particular topic. The Bible is the source of everything that God wants us to know so we can be the people that He wants us to be.

But if more information is the goal of your message, then you have let your people down. The reason that God wants us to have more biblical information is so we will live more biblical lives. You are not preaching a sermon to prepare your people for a theological exam. You are preaching the Bible to prepare them for life.

When Jesus preached the Beatitudes in the Sermon on the Mount (Matthew 5:3-12), His aim was not just that we would have more *information* about being meek, or more *knowledge* about being merciful, or a better *understanding* of what it meant to be pure in heart. He proclaimed this message so that we would **become** more meek, more merciful and more pure in heart. His destination wasn't just a knowledge change, it was a life change!

When Jesus told the story of "The Good Samaritan" (Luke 10:30-37) – He didn't tell us so we would just better understand the socio-political situation of the Jews and the Samaritans. Nor did he relate this story just to give us a better theology of what it meant to be merciful. The destination of His message was that we would become more merciful! You can see this clearly in how the message concludes:

"Which of these three do you think was a neighbour to the man who fell into the hands of robbers?" The expert in the law replied, "The one who had mercy on him." Jesus told him, **"Go and do likewise."**   **Luke 10:36-37**

The destination of any impactful message is **life change.** If people are not challenged to change their life in light of what God has taught them in that message, then their destination will be a very second-rate one.

2. "I feel different"
The destination of emotion

Ever had to listen to a boring sermon? Ever *preached* a boring sermon? You know what it's like when the preacher drones on and on, and you have no idea why you should even keep listening. It makes sense that many Bible teachers have determined *"I will never bore anyone like that"*. It is entirely reasonable that many good Bible teachers have become experts in story-telling, humorous anecdotes, gripping illustrations and compelling challenges. Nothing wrong with all that. Way to go!

But that is not the destination! The aim of the message is not to help people feel differently. The aim is to help them live differently. I can feel all sorts of pain and sympathy as I look at pictures of starving kids around the world, but if I don't change my life to do something about it, then all that emotion – genuine as it is – has been pointless. I can feel sorry for my sins, but unless I turn from them in repentance, all my sorrow has simply been self-serving.

My colleagues in the secular professional speaking world are at a turning point on this issue. I hear things like this from my professional colleagues:

"People aren't listening to you because they want your knowledge.

If they just want your information, they can google you. The question you need to ask at the end of any speech is this 'Did I make my audience feel something?'"

I understand the reason for this – and I understand the passion with which they say it. And I know that a lot of audience members will be well satisfied if they simply feel something during your message. We live in a world where so many people are desperate to feel anything. They will pay good money to go to films, theatres, concerts and sporting events because they simply want to feel something. They will watch a romantic movie because they want to rekindle emotions of love; they will watch a comedy because they want to laugh; they will watch a horror movie because they want to be scared out of their wits; they will attend a concert because they want to be entertained and uplifted; they will join the masses at a sporting event because they simply want to feel passion once again.

Nothing wrong with any of these emotions – **but the emotion is not the destination**. A great message will heighten people's emotions so that they are more determined to change their life to fit in with God's master plan. You don't get on a train because you want to feel something; you get on a train because there's a destination you want to reach.

3. "I'm ready to change my life"
The destination of transformation
I believe that this is the only destination worth taking people to. Every time I preach to Christians, I want to take them on a journey through God's word so that they will change some aspect of the way they live. Every time I speak to the non-Christian kids at our youth group, I want to take them on a journey towards Christ so that they will stop living for themselves and submit their whole lives to Jesus.

This "destination of transformation" is not reserved just for sermons and Bible talks. This is the best destination for **any** speech! When I speak at a wedding, I don't just want to say nice things about the bride and groom; I want to urge them to be even more authentic and open in their relationship than they were thinking of. As a sporting coach, when I address my football team at half-time – and the score-line is against us – I don't just want them to have more information about the opposition's weaknesses. I don't just want them to be more motivated to "give 110%". They might well need to know both these things – but the destination I am after is life-change. That is, I want them to play the second half differently from how they played the first half.

Let's just pause so that we can all take a breath. Here's where we've got to so far:

1. **Every message you preach should take people on a journey**
2. **Every message you preach should take people to a destination**
3. **That destination is always *transformation***

So far, so good? Now let's tackle the really key question – "How?"

Chapter 4

Every journey needs a plan

No matter what journey you take, you need a plan. If you're driving, it might be a street directory, a roadmap or a GPS. If you're travelling by plane, bus or train, you might need a timetable, a route map, and information about arrivals. A journey is something which is intentional. There is a plan at the beginning, a destination at the end – and a carefully devised route that will get you there. Even if you allow for flexibility along the way, there still has to be a plan for your ultimate destination, and maybe even your return trip!

Of course, you can start travelling without a plan. But don't call that a journey. That's just wandering. You just set out and see where you'll end up.

When my sister and I were young children, we would often go for a walk together. We often didn't have much of a plan. We just wandered – following whatever caught our eye. One day we set off for an afternoon walk, and our total "plan" was: *Take the first street on the right; then take the first turn on the left; then the next turn on the right* … It was fun; it was interesting; but it wasn't a journey. We didn't arrive at any particular destination. We were just wandering.

Nothing wrong with wandering, but don't do it when you're at the lectern. Then everyone else is forced to meander around with you as well. And believe me, I've heard enough messages from "wanderers without plans", where they seemed to proclaim whatever came into their mind on the spur of the moment. If you want to have a verbal wander, then do it by yourself, when no-one is watching (or listening!). But don't drag a room full of people along with you. Start with a plan, and take them to a destination that is worth arriving at!

Here is the roadmap that I will use for the remainder of our journey. I want to divide our excursion into four distinct stages[1]:

1. The Hook
2. The Book
3. The Look
4. The Took

I am not pretending that every message spoken in the Bible follows this structure. Nor am I suggesting that every preacher in the world should follow this slavishly. But if you're learning the art of preaching or giving talks, or if you're a seasoned Bible teacher and you want to be more effective in what you do, then it is a great model to work with. I use this model myself – and I teach it to hundreds of others around the world.

Here's a quick overview. I will give you all the details in the rest of the book.

1. The Hook

This is where every good message starts. **How will I get my passengers on the train?** Because if you don't "hook" your passengers – if you don't engage them right at the beginning – if you can't persuade your passengers to leave the comfort of the departure lounge and get on board with you, then you will not take anyone on a journey that day. You might have a wonderful

---

1   This structure was originally developed and expounded by Larry Richards in his 1970 book (revised 1998) *Creative Bible Teaching (Moody Publishers)*.

trip, but it will be all by yourself. Not one of your listeners will arrive at their destination.

2. The Book

This is the biblical information which will control every other part of the journey. This is where you dive into God's revealed word to show what He wants us to know. The faithful preacher is not making up their own message; the faithful preacher is not deciding on their own destination; the faithful preacher is submitting themselves to God's word and relying on Him to reveal the message that He wants us to hear. It is the biblical material that will determine the destination. It is the biblical material which will over-ride the "Hook", the "Look" and the "Took". The beginning, middle and the end of the message will be determined by what God says in the Bible. The destination will always be one that God reveals.

3. The Look

This is the exploration that you will do to help people discover the truths revealed in God's word. What stories will you tell that will help your audience see the wonders in God's word? What illustrations can you paint with your words to help bring out the true spiritual meaning of the text?

This is where the craft of the teacher comes to the fore. Having done the hard work to nail down what God's word is actually saying (the Book), in this section (the Look), you will explain and illustrate God's word clearly so it is riveted on the hearts of each member of your congregation.

4. The Took

This is what your audience will take with them as you conclude. This is your destination. This is your application. This is the take-home message that you want everyone to leave with. This is what you want to be ringing in everyone's ears. The Took is where you will make it clear what the life-changing moment is in this whole journey. This is what makes the journey worthwhile. Without the Took, all anyone has is information. Good information, maybe, but mere information. Unless this information has been converted into action, then the journey was not worth the effort. The Took is the practical bit that many people will find the most helpful.

I have presented these four stages in a certain order, because that is roughly the order that a great Bible talk will follow. Not precisely, but more or less. Here is what definitely is true:

The Hook will be at the beginning and the Took will be at the end. You have to have a start – and a finish – with any good message. These two servants will do this job marvellously! But that is not the *only* place where they will be used.

The Hook will be used at any time in the message where the passengers are likely to get off the train. Depending on your audience, you may need to use a hook at many times throughout your message. Unless your passengers are convinced to stay on your train, then you will not take anyone to the destination on that day.

I preach extensively to teenagers – and I love them, and they are brilliant – but sometimes they are harder to convince that your destination is worth arriving at! I will use hooks at any part of the message where I anticipate that my audience runs the risk of being disengaged.

Similarly, even though you will use the Took to conclude your message, there's no reason why your application can't be spread throughout your talk. If you have three major points in your plan, it is entirely possible that you will want to have a Took enmeshed in each of your three points. It's always great to have a strong challenge at the end – but there's no reason why your message can't be challenging throughout.

In the same way, your Book and your Look will be intertwined throughout your whole plan. In the main part of your talk, you might go back and forth between "Book" and "Look" as you teach various parts of your message. The order that I have placed them in suggests that you investigate the Book before you go off on excursions with your Look, but sometimes it can be fun to reverse this completely!

> *So, if you understand the four key sections,*
> *how do you actually plan your message?*
> *How do you prepare your journey?*

Chapter 5

Preparing the journey

E very worthwhile journey needs thorough preparation. Your preparation comes before your journey commences. Long before you stand up and preach; way before you start writing your message; even before you start thinking of stories, anecdotes and killer-endings; you need to plan the journey so you take all your passengers to the right destination.

Here are the three key questions to ask:

1.   **What is my message?**
2.   **Why would my listeners want to hear this?**
3.   **What is my destination?**

Let's check out all three. There is more information on all this in later chapters. But right now, let's have a quick overview of how to plan the whole thing.

1. What is my message?
This will determine your Book

Before you say anything in your Bible talk, you need to work out what it is that you will say. Unlike a speech at any other event, a sermon is always controlled by what God has said in the Bible. So whatever your message, you need to first work out what God is actually saying.

Have you ever heard a Bible talk where the speaker left out this step? They might have had compelling stories; they may well have had some great information. But deep down, they never came to terms with God's word; they never understood their biblical passage; so they never discovered the God-given destination that had been planned for them.

Coming to terms with the Book is vital, because it is the Book that will control and determine your Hook, your Look and your Took. I want to suggest now that you will struggle to move on to the rest of your preparation until you have worked out what God's Word is actually saying. You'll find all the clues to this in the next section.

2. Why would my listeners want to hear this?
This will determine your Hook and your Look

I fear that this question is rarely asked. So many preachers – having discovered what God's word is saying in the Bible – having determined their three main points and their application at the end – never stop and ask the question: *"Why would anyone in my audience want to hear this?"*

I heard a sermon recently about the character of God. The speaker carefully showed us how God is all-powerful, all-knowing, and present everywhere (*omnipotent, omniscient and omnipresent*). All good stuff. Faithful Bible handling. But here was the problem: *The speaker had never asked **why** their listeners needed to hear this.* I suspect that most people already believed these three main points before the preacher even began. There were no false teachers running around the congregation proclaiming that God wasn't all powerful, or wasn't all knowing, or wasn't present everywhere. Most of the listeners had believed all these things since birth.

So why did this message need to be taught? Possibly it might have been that some people in the church were *living* as if God were not fully in charge; or believing that they could hide things from God, or not trusting God to lead them every step of the way. **That's why the message needed to be preached.**

If you never work out why your listeners need to hear your

message, then you will never engage them on the journey. So as soon as you have determined the **what** (*what does the passage actually say?*), make sure you determine the **why** (*why does this congregation need to hear this?*).

3. What is my destination?
This will determine your Took

Before you start your journey as a train-driving preacher, you need to know what your single, unique destination is. You need to know where you're heading. You need to know where you want to take all your passengers. You need to know what you want to be ringing in their heads at the end of your message. You need to know what is the life change that you will be driving for.

In one sense, your Took will be determined by your Book. The Bible passage itself will guide you to the life change that God requires. And it may well be that as your preparation continues, you discover that what you *thought* was the final destination – is indeed just a staging post, and that God has revealed to you in his word what the true destination really is.

Here is why I want to work out my destination right at the beginning of my preparation. Your Took will heavily influence what your Hook will be. That is, a great start to your journey is one that links it in with your destination. If your message is truly integrated, your Took will answer the question that is raised in your Hook.

Here's an example: I was preaching on Easter Day from Luke 24:13-32 (The Road to Emmaus).

The big picture: Jesus has risen from the dead – and He appears to his disciples to encourage and instruct them.

The destination: This answers the question: *so what?* That is, if Jesus has risen from the dead, what difference should this make to me now? How is my life meant to be different? Anyway, here is the destination that seemed right to me: **that whatever you**

are facing at the moment, the risen Lord is there to give you hope.

The Hook: The destination (above) heavily influenced my Hook right at the beginning. My message started with the words: *"Have you ever had one of those times in your life – when you had your heart set on something – and all your hopes were dashed to pieces?"* Hopefully this engaged most of my listeners, but more importantly – my Hook was determined by my Took. That is, the question I raised right at the beginning of the message, was answered in my application at the end.

A word of warning about preparation:

When you are presenting a message, this is the rough order of these four key stages:

1. **The Hook**
2. **The Book**
3. **The Look**
4. **The Took**

But that is not the order in which you will do your preparation! When you sit down to think through your upcoming message, **don't start with the Hook!** If you start with the Hook, then you will lose your biblical perspective. You will find that your Hook dominates the whole message and in the end dictates your destination. You will end up preaching a man-made message with a man-made destination.

You know how easy it is to fall into this trap. You've heard a great story. It's funny; it's engaging; it has a killer punch-line – and you are *desperate* to get it into the first message you can. And so you design and plan your whole Bible talk based on this opening story.

Can I suggest to you that is not what God wants? He wants His Book to control your message. **He doesn't want your message**

to control His Book! God Himself has a message for you to teach; He has a destination in mind for you to take your listeners to; He wants His word in His scriptures to control not only your whole life, but your every message.

So for the purposes of this book, I have arranged the four stages of your journey **in the order in which you will prepare them.** This is to make sure we all start with the important bit first. So the layout for the rest of the book goes like this:

1. **The Book** (*yes – this stage always comes first in your preparation, and includes identifying the Hook and the Took*)
2. **The Hook**
3. **The Look**
4. **The Took**

> *But before you prepare the journey,*
> *you need to prepare the train-driver.*

Chapter 6

Preparing the train driver

People sometimes ask me:
"How long did it take you to prepare that message?"
My normal answer is:
"Around thirty-five years."

That's how long I have been in full-time ministry. I have been a Christian for around forty years. Perhaps that would be a more accurate answer to the question! Indeed, I have been on this planet for around sixty years. And for all that time, God keeps working through all things in my life to produce a Christ-like result.

"And we know that in all things God works for the good of those who love him, who have been called according to his purpose." **Romans 8:28**

Teaching God's message to others is like nothing else on this planet; because I can never divorce who I am in Christ from what I do for Christ. Indeed, I cannot make any real claim for what I am doing for Christ – because my life is a testament to what Christ is doing in me. The greatest preparation you will do for any message that you will present is to devote yourself to a lifetime of having your heart prepared by God's word. God is far more interested in the work He is doing in you, rather than the work He is doing through you. Because the work He is doing in you is what will be reproduced into the hearts of your listeners.

Every now and then, like a kick in the teeth, God challenges me in an area of my life where I have been neglecting Him. Maybe He calls me to return to His word; perhaps He beckons me back to be a man of prayer; He might challenge me in an area of my behaviour where I have drifted into disobedience; He keeps calling me to be more worshipful, more generous, more forgiving ... and as I look back over my years, I can see the points where God has challenged me in a new way to be His man. I can look back at significant decisions I have made to be more Christlike in all that I do. Those of you who know me will readily acknowledge that I still have a lot of work to do! I know I am not yet the man that God wants me to be. But I praise God that I am no longer the man I used to be!

Here's the thing I have noticed at every one of these points of repentance in my life: whenever I turn back to Jesus in a significant way – *my preaching gets better.* More passionate. More faithful. More insightful. More transparent. More genuine. More effective. I have discovered, the hard and painful way, that the best thing I can ever do for my preaching is to make sure that the first person I preach to is myself. Just before I go and apply God's word to the teeming masses, I need to apply it to me.

God has called you to be a spiritual train driver. He is giving you a destination to take His people to. He is preparing a journey for you, and showing you the way ahead.

Here is the key to understanding all this. This is the most helpful piece of advice anyone has ever given me about preaching. This is the most significant factor in how effective your teaching will be. You can have all the preaching techniques in the world, but without this vital step, your words will be hollow, and your destination meaningless.

This advice can be said in a number of ways. But deep down they

all mean the same thing. Read each of the following statements –
slowly – and apply each one to your own journey.

Before you build the hearts of the people,
you need to build the heart of the preacher.
Before you prepare the journey,
you need to prepare the train-driver.

If you want God's word to be effective in your congregation,
then God's word must be effective in your life.

Who you are in Christ,
will speak more powerfully than what you say for Christ.

Your people don't expect you to be God.
But they do expect that you will constantly meet with him.

The preacher is like the driver at the front of the train.
When the preacher stays on track, everyone gets to the right
destination.

But when the preacher gets off the track, everyone gets derailed. Here
are the things that I have discovered that keep my heart on track.

1. Be immersed in God's word

The first step to being an effective preacher, is to remember that
God's word first has to be preached to you. You are not preparing
a message just to change and challenge everyone else; the first
person to be changed and challenged should be you.

In Romans 2, Paul is firing a broadside at the Jewish leaders
because they had abandoned this very principle. As you read these
words aimed at the religious leaders of the day, apply them to your
own heart:

... If you are convinced that you are a guide for the blind, a light for those who are in the dark, an instructor of the foolish, a teacher of little children, because you have in the law the embodiment of knowledge and truth—you, then, who teach others, do you not teach yourself? You who preach against stealing, do you steal? You who say that people should not commit adultery, do you commit adultery? You who abhor idols, do you rob temples? You who boast in the law, do you dishonour God by breaking the law? As it is written: "God's name is blasphemed among the Gentiles because of you."   **Romans 2:19-24**

Wouldn't it be terrible if God's name were blasphemed by those outside of Christ, because a Christian preacher was caught out for not practising what they preached? You know this has happened. Will you join me in making a commitment that it will never happen *because of me*?

2. Be immersed in prayer

I love how Jesus says:

"Apart from me you can do nothing."   **John 15:5**

He doesn't say:
   "Apart from me you might be a little less effective."
   "Apart from me your preaching might be a little less powerful."
   "Apart from me you will not preach to such large numbers of people."

He says:

"Apart from me you can do nothing."

When I was in my early days as a youth pastor, I was excitedly preparing a new message on the subject of prayer. I researched it thoroughly; I investigated all the possibilities; I checked out all my references; and I carefully planned the delivery.

Halfway through my preparation, God jolted my mind with a devastating thought: *I haven't even prayed about it!* How is that possible? How could I be preparing a message on the very topic of prayer – and neglect to even offer *one prayer* to ask for God's help and guidance? Aarrgghh!!

If I do not approach preaching with a heart of prayer, then I will take my audience on a merely human journey to a merely human destination. Do you want to be a great preacher? Then learn to be a great pray-er.

Just before I preach, my mind is running in a thousand directions. *Is my mic turned on? Have I got all my notes? Have I set my stopwatch? What was my opening line again? Is this the last verse of the song?* In the middle of this turmoil, I have disciplined myself to pray. I am always praying just before I step up to preach. I might not look like it, but I can assure you that I am. And at that point, I can never think of any brilliant words to craft a prayer of huge eloquence. I can tell you the prayer I will be praying any time just before I teach God's word. This has been my prayer for the last thirty five years – and it will continue to be so. I commend it to you.

Here it is. I say to God: *Not me, but you.* A short prayer. A simple prayer. But I say it over and over again. Because that's exactly what I want. I don't want my preaching to be all about me – and my abilities. I want it to be all about God – and His abilities.

Do you want to stand on your feet as a great preacher? Then prepare on your knees.

3. Stay in step with God's Spirit

The brilliant thing about teaching God's word – or any ministry at all – is that we don't have to do it in our own strength. God's Holy Spirit is there to strengthen us, to guide us, and to empower us for faithful and effective ministry.

The following words were spoken by Jesus when His disciples did not know what they would do if they were arrested and hauled before the authorities. As you hear His message to them, apply it to your own life, where Jesus calls you into a new and scary situation.

> "But when they arrest you, do not worry about what to say or how to say it. At that time you will be given what to say, for it will not be you speaking, but the Spirit of your Father speaking through you.
>
> **Matthew 10:19-20**

This is not an argument against preparing well, or using notes, or practising your message. The simple truth is this: it will not be you speaking but the Spirit of your Father speaking through you.

God's Holy Spirit is there to guide you, equip you, empower you and comfort you. Trust yourself to your heavenly Father and prepare your heart to speak with spiritual authenticity and authority.

4. Keep unwrapping the Spirit's gifts

The ability to teach God's word is an ability that comes from God. It is a spiritual gift that God gives to some so that they can activate the gifts within the people of God so that the whole body grows.

> So Christ Himself gave the apostles, the prophets, the evangelists, the **pastors and teachers**, to equip God's people for works of service, so that the body of Christ may be built up.
>
> **Ephesians 4:11-12**

Every Christian is gifted by God's Spirit to exercise a ministry to help the whole body grow. Some are given gifts of teaching. That means, if God has called you to teach His word to others, then He has also equipped you to do it.

But like any gift you receive, you need to unwrap it and activate it for it to be of any use. Paul says to Timothy:

For this reason I remind you to fan into flame the gift of God, which is in you through the laying on of my hands.
                                                                              2 Timothy 1:6

So keep unwrapping the Spirit's gifts. Move forward in the strength with which God is equipping you for any ministry that He is calling you to. But make sure you fan it into flame: strive to be the very best you can be at whatever ministry God has called you to.

Of course, not everyone who wants to preach has been called by God to do it. Not everyone who attempts to give a Bible talk has been gifted by God in this way. How do you know whether you have this gift?

At some point *it needs to be recognised by God's people.* When you have taught the Bible to others – whether it is one- on one, or in a Bible-study group, or in front of a large audience – what feedback do people give you afterwards? If they keep telling you how much God's word has impacted their life, or how clearly they now understand what the Bible says, or they thank you for challenging them on a key issue, then that is the body of Christ recognising the gifts God has given you.

On the other hand, if people's reaction is more likely to be *total avoidance* – or if people tend to say: *Have you thought about trying another ministry?* – then that might give you the clue that God could be preparing you for a more effective ministry elsewhere.

5. One last warning

> Not many of you should presume to be teachers, my
> brothers, because you know that we who teach will be
> judged more strictly.   **James 3:1**

Teaching God's word is a powerful ministry. And yet if it is done badly, or you teach the wrong thing, or you guide people in the wrong way – it is potentially extremely damaging. That's why God's word teaches us to be careful. Because if I teach God's word badly, I don't just risk bringing myself down – I risk bringing down my hearers as well.

The preacher is like the driver at the front of the train.
When the preacher stays on track, everyone gets to the right
   destination.
But when the preacher gets off the track, everyone gets derailed.

This whole book is to help you to prepare your teaching faithfully, and to deliver your message effectively. But do not neglect the most important preparation of all – to first prepare your own heart to be both faithful and effective.

Chapter 7

The importance of the Bible

This is the most important stage. Your Book controls your whole message. Your biblical information influences your Hook, your Look and your Took. It determines your destination and controls your whole journey. Your careful work in understanding and explaining the great message of the Bible will point your listeners to the God-given change He wants in their life as they arrive at His God-given destination.

We live in a world that will readily discard God's word to the rubbish heap of ancient irrelevant beliefs. Indeed, there are modern movements in preaching that treat the Bible as nothing more than a collection of stories and illustrations.

Can we pause for a moment to remind ourselves of the absolute power of God's written word?

1. It's powerful

For the word of God is living and active. Sharper than any double-edged sword, it penetrates even to dividing soul and spirit, joints and marrow; it judges the thoughts and attitudes of the heart. Nothing in all creation is hidden from God's sight. Everything is uncovered and laid bare before the eyes of him to whom we must give account.

Hebrews 4:12-13

It's easy to think of the Bible as something that is primarily designed to sit on the shelf. To gather dust. Or, for the more digitally inclined, an app that you download to your mobile device, but only use on the rare occasions when you can't connect to Facebook.

God's word is nothing like that. It is not a passive resting place for weary dust mites nor a catalogue of heart-warming thoughts suitable for daily calendar quotes. God Himself describes His word as being *alive and active*. God's word is a razor-sharp sword that will slice into our inner being. It will penetrate our lives; it will discern our thoughts; it will judge our attitudes. The Bible is like a far-ranging searchlight that invades every nook and cranny and reveals every hiding place. And it exposes the people who are hiding there! God's word is like an invincible wrestler who overpowers anyone who stands in the way – and lays them out – conquered, naked, exposed and vulnerable.

That's powerful stuff! And that is the power that the preacher unleashes when they open God's word to their listeners.

God's word has always been powerful. With His word, God created an entire universe (Genesis 1). When God's word took on flesh in the person of Jesus, the biggest act of redemption and rescue was put into place. God's written word is no different. Through it lives are changed; hearts are renewed; eternities are set.

That's why the Bible has to control *everything* you say as a Bible teacher.

2. It meets our every need
If all you had was the forceful picture in Hebrews 4, you could perhaps be excused for thinking that God's word served no other purpose than to knock us off our collective perches and pull us down into the mire at the bottom of the cage.

Far from it. God's word is the *only* answer for everything that we so desperately need. Every cry of our heart; every tear in our eye; every ache of our existence – God's word provides the soothing balm which takes us to the glorious destination that God has designed for us.

Look at this short selection from Psalm 19:

The law of the LORD is perfect, reviving the soul.
The statutes of the LORD are trustworthy,
> making wise the simple.
The precepts of the LORD are right, giving joy to the heart.
The commands of the LORD are radiant,
> giving light to the eyes.   **Psalm 19:7-8**

They are more precious than gold, than much pure gold;
they are sweeter than honey, than honey from the
> honeycomb.
By them is your servant warned;
> in keeping them there is great reward." **Psalm 19:10-11**

Do you want to help refresh people's souls? Do you want to give them true wisdom? Do you want to bring joy to people's hearts? Do you want to give light to their eyes? This will never be achieved by our fine preaching and skilful oratory. This will only be achieved by getting our lives into God's Word, and getting God's word into our lives.

Here are some of the most well-known verses about the powerful effect of God's word.

All Scripture is God-breathed and is useful for teaching,
rebuking, correcting and training in righteousness, so that
the servant of God may be thoroughly equipped for every
good work.   **2 Timothy 3:16-17**

We'll get back to the "God-breathed" bit in a moment. Did you note **what God's word will do for you?** It will teach you. It will rebuke you. It will train you for righteousness. It will thoroughly equip you for every good work. *That's* the destination that God wants to take every one of His servants to. And His word is the only vehicle that will get you there. That's why in every sermon you preach; in every message that you teach; for every journey you take your hearers on – God's word will not only dictate what your destination is, but it is the only thing that will take you and your listeners to that destination.

And why is that?

3. It is the word of God Himself

Every thought that I can imagine is a man-made thought. Every word that I say is a man-made word. Every idea that I conceive is a man-made idea. Not bad within themselves… but if all I give my hearers are man-made thoughts, man-made words and man-made ideas, then I can only take them to a man-made destination.

This is what separates the Bible from every other writing from every age of civilization. Every other publication (even this worthy tome!) is the word of a failed and fragile human. Only the Bible is the word of God Himself.

All Scripture is God-breathed…   **2 Timothy 3:16**

The Bible is not a collection of thoughts about God. It is not the pinnacle of human penmanship on all things theological. The words of the Bible are the very words of God Himself. *"All Scripture is God-breathed"* tells us that every single word in the Bible is breathed out by God himself.

We often use the word *"inspire"* to describe God's relationship with His Bible. (*"God inspired the Bible"*). I know what people mean by this. I use this term myself. But *inspire* means **to breathe in**. The word for *breathe out* is *expire*.

2 Timothy 3:16 doesn't tell us that all Scripture is breathed in by God. What this amazing verse tells us is that all Scripture is *breathed out* by God. If you do not let God's word control every part of your preaching journey, you run the risk of taking all your passengers to a man-made destination.

The Bible is not the word of humans. It is the word of God:

And we also thank God continually because, when you received the word of God, which you heard from us, you accepted it not as a human word, but as it actually is, the word of God, which is indeed at work in you who believe.

1 Thessalonians 2:13

Above all, you must understand that no prophecy of Scripture came about by the prophet's own interpretation of things. For prophecy never had its origin in the will of man, but prophets spoke from God as they were carried along by the Holy Spirit. **2 Peter 1:20-21**

The only way to take your passengers to a God-given destination is to ensure that your message is totally controlled by God-given words.

4. So... handle with care

Do your best to present yourself to God as one approved, a worker who does not need to be ashamed and who correctly handles the word of truth." **2 Timothy 2:15**

In the Bible, the role of a leader is never separated from the role of a Bible teacher. When we look through the four New Testament lists of what is required in a Christian leader (1 Timothy 3:1-7, 1 Timothy 3:8-13, 2 Timothy 2:22-26, Titus 1:5-9), there is only one skill or ability mentioned. That they be *able to teach*. To teach God's word as skilled craftsmen.

There is a warning here to those of us who teach the Bible. We need to handle God's word with care. It is a powerful weapon. It brings light to those in darkness; it brings hope to those in despair; it brings life to those who are dead. If we are aiming to take people on a journey to a destination that we believe is worthwhile, then we need to make sure that we are operating as skilled craftsmen – trusted workers – correctly handling the word of truth.

We need to make sure that the message that we preach is indeed the message that God wants us to preach. We need to double-check that what we're explaining from the Bible is indeed what the Bible is actually saying. We need to make sure that the message we are proclaiming is the same message that God wants us to proclaim. We need to make sure that we fit our message around the Bible, rather than fitting the Bible around our message.

So – how do we do that?
Next chapter!

Chapter 8

How to prepare a Bible message

I f you're preparing to preach a sermon or present a Bible-talk, – then this is the place to start. Why? Because you want to make sure that the Bible controls everything else in your message!

Your Book will control your Hook, your Look and your Took. Here's the principle: **get your message right first!** Then you can work out how to say it.

There are no unbreakable laws of nature that dictate how you should prepare a talk. But here are the steps which I have found immensely valuable. These are the steps that I take to help ensure that the message I come up with is indeed a faithful representation of the message that God speaks in the Bible.

1. If you want God's help – ask Him

There's no rocket science in suggesting that you should start your preparation in prayer. But there have been so many times in my life where I have been so *gung-ho* to get into my message that I have overlooked this vital first step!

To put it quite simply: if you want God to guide and steer you on this exciting journey; if you want His empowerment in putting this message together; if you want to ensure that your teaching is faithful to the original meaning of the Bible; if you want to keep your heart humble and obedient as you embark on this adventure; if you want to take your people to the correct destination – the one that God Himself has indeed determined – then stop and ask for God's help in prayer. Bathe the whole process in prayer. Trust in God every step of the way.

2. Read and re-read the passage

If you have been given a Bible passage to teach from – read it. If you need to select your own, then go on – select it. Then read the passage. Read it again. Read what comes before it. Read what comes after it. If you are preaching from an individual verse – or a selection of verses – do the same. Read and re-read them all. Read them in their contexts. Read them swiftly. Read them slowly. Read them in a few different translations. Read where it fits in its chapter in the Bible. Read where it fits in its book in the Bible.

If you understand some Greek or Hebrew, then read it in its original languages. But at this stage don't go to commentaries or other books that might explain the Bible. Not yet, anyway. Trust in God and read it for yourself. I never want to check with someone else's thoughts until I have wrestled with the passage myself.

If you need more help in working out: *What does this passage really say? What does it really mean?* then have a look through my checklist in the next chapter.

3. Re-write the passage

One of the best ways I have ever found to discover for myself what the Bible is actually saying, is to rewrite it – verse by verse. My rewriting sticks pretty closely to the original. Often I will summarise verses a little. I want to check that I understand each verse. I want to understand how each verse connects with the next verse. I want to get a handle on the flow of the passage. I wrestle with each verse until I think I have a basic understanding of why it is there and how it contributes to the overall journey.

At this point I'm not looking for deep meaning. I'm not trying to interpret each verse or apply it too much. I'm just trying to work out: *Can I understand what each verse is saying, and how it all leads to a destination?*

4. What's the big idea?

As I re-read and re-write the passage, I'm trying to work out: *What's the big idea?* That is, what's the overall destination of these verses? What's the one point they are making? What is one sentence or one thought or one statement that sums up everything? Sometimes this *big idea* will come easily. At other times it will be a bit of a struggle. But I keep asking myself this question: *Based on what I have just read, what is the big message that God wants to give to His people?*

I will wrestle with this until I get it. Sometimes, after I have dug into the passage a bit deeper, this *big idea* might change a little. I might realise that my initial summary was a little shallow, or picked up on a secondary point, or needs to be sharpened or clarified. But at this early stage, I want to get a handle on what I think the big idea is.

I find I can't move forward until I've settled on this. And here's why: the *big idea* will determine your destination. It will give you the finishing point for your journey. It will show you what to aim at. It will tell you where to take your passengers. Once you've got the big idea in mind, you have answered the first question of any good train driver: *Where do we want to be?* Or I guess, strictly speaking, the correct question here is *Where does **God** want us to be?*

It is vital to work out the *big idea* right at the very start, because that will define your destination.

5. Can I divide it into some main sub-points?

I then try to work out whether there are any obvious main sub-points along the way. Are there any places where the Scripture moves on to the *next step* in its argument? I wrestle with the passage until I can subdivide it into the obvious steps it seems to take.

This is an important stage because it determines the stations you will most probably call at on your journey. And each point on the adventure should prepare you for the next point on your travels. That is, if your listeners will follow you to your first station, what is it about that first station that will make them want to travel to the second station as well?

Once again, sometimes this subdivision is dead obvious. The passage almost *preaches itself.* At other times I can't work out the main points at all! Sometimes there will appear to be at least two different ways of subdividing the passage. Keep working it through until you have a reasonable outline of the journey that you will take.

6. Check the insight of other people

Once you have done all this preliminary work, then you can check what others think. If you have a trusted friend, now is the time to ask for their opinion. If you want to check the commentaries or study guides, now would be the time. Here are some of the times when I have found a commentary helpful: when I haven't been able to work out what a verse means; when I haven't been able to get a decent picture of the overall idea; when I can't quite see how it divides into sub-points; if there are words or phrases that sound confusing. Remember, a commentary is only another human being's opinion – so weigh it carefully before adopting it. And do check out that you are getting your information from a trusted source – especially if you are going online!

The following points refer more to working out your Hook, Look and Took, and there's plenty of more info on this in other chapters. But right now is a good time to ask some of the key questions.

7. Ask the question: *So what?*

Once you have worked out your overall message, try and ask the question *So what?* That is, if everything you have looked at is true, what difference is it meant to make? How is my life meant to be different because of what God has just taught me? How might God want the lives of my listeners to be challenged as a result of this biblical journey?

This *So what?* question is absolutely vital. Without it, your message might just fill people's heads with mere information. Your *So what* question will start to define your application. If the ultimate destination is *Transformation*, then this question will further refine the climax of your journey. Your *So what?* question will start to clarify your Took.

Of course, your application might get far more precise once you are getting close to the finish of your preparation. But I like to get a reasonable idea of what the application will be for this reason: it will clarify both the start and the finish of your message. It will help you to know more precisely *where* you will finish your journey with your passengers. But it will also help you establish your *starting point.* That is, when you know what your final challenge is for *behaviour change,* (your Took), then you will know what question to ask to determine how you engage your passengers right at the start (your Hook).

8. Ask the question:
Why would anyone want to listen?

Here are the three vital steps you have worked out already:

- Your overall Bible message (your Book)
- The main sub-points (which will become your Look)
- The main behaviour-change application at the end (your Took)

Once you have worked out these three vital steps... then you are ready to formulate your Hook. Why would your audience want to listen to this? Can you work out the resistance point that your listeners might have taking this message on board? Where at the moment are they getting it wrong? What is going on in their world that will make this message difficult for them to live out?

Chapter 9 will show you the key questions to ask of the Bible text itself. The subsequent chapters will show you how to work on your Hook, your Look and your Took. But I always like to try and answer the *So what?* and the *Why would anyone want to listen?* questions right at the beginning of my preparation.

Getting the Bible message right

I hope you have picked up by now how important the Bible message is. Getting it right is absolutely crucial. Otherwise you might end up proclaiming a message that is different from God's message in the Bible.

This book is not meant to be an exhaustive investigation of preaching skills such as "exegesis", "hermeneutics" and "homiletics". There are far weightier tomes than this which will take you to profound depth on all these subjects. But here are three questions to help you home in on the core message that God wants you to understand and share with your hearers:

1. What does the passage really say?

This one requires a bit of work. But it really matters. You can't just jump to a passage and guess what it's saying! What it means **now** has to be consistent with what it meant **when it was first written**.

Follow these guidelines to help you get it right:

- What did the original writer say to the original readers?
- Read and re-read it **yourself**.
- Wrestle it through on your own.

Remember, at this point you're not trying to work out what the passage really means. You're simply trying to work out *What does it actually **say**?*

Here are some things that you'll need to take into account:

a. The background
- Who wrote it?
- To whom was it written?
- Why was it written?

You can often find out these answers by reading the context – going back to the beginning of the book – or sometimes you might need to refer to a commentary so that you understand the original setting.

b. The context
- What comes immediately before and after the passage?
- How does the passage fit into the book as a whole?
- How does the passage fit into the Bible as a whole?

Never just grab a verse by itself and interpret it without reading the passages that come before and after it. I remember what my old Bible-college principal used to say: *"A text without a context is a pretext"*.

c. The style of literature
Different sorts of literature will present things in different ways. How you understand a historical section of the Bible (eg: Acts) will be different from how you understand a part of the Bible that is a song (eg: Psalms).

So what sort of literature is it? You might need to check with some commentaries to help you know how to understand it correctly.

Is it history, prose, poetry, proverb, allegory, parable, letter, prophecy, narrative, soliloquy, dialogue, apocalyptic... ?

d. What do the words and phrases mean?

The original Bible was mainly written in Hebrew (Old Testament) and Greek (New Testament). What does the original language really mean? You don't need to be a language scholar to get this right! Simply check out your verse in a number of different good English translations. This will help you to check that you're not misunderstanding a verse.

2. What does the passage really mean?

Now that you've worked out what the passage actually says to the original readers, you can take the second step, which is to determine: *What did the passage really **mean** to the original readers?*

Check these out:

- How are today's hearers different or similar to the original hearers?
- How is the world situation today different or similar to the society it was originally written to?
- Look for the parallels!

If you've done your hard work back in the *What does the passage really say?* section, then the passage's meaning will probably fall into place a little easier.

Let's imagine you are speaking from Psalm 98. What do you make of this verse?

Sing to the LORD a new song, for he has done marvellous things; his right hand and his holy arm have worked salvation for him. **Psalm 98:1**

If you ask the question: *What does the passage really say?*, your answer might be something like:

- We should praise God
- Because He has done great things
- His right hand and holy arm have worked salvation for Him

Then you look at the end of that verse, and ask the question: *What does it mean – "his right hand and his holy arm"?*

Does this mean that God literally has one right hand and one holy arm? Does it mean that God actually has arms and hands at all? Are you starting to see where the question *What does it mean?* goes slightly deeper than your original question *What does it say?*

You might want to find out where else the Bible uses the terms *"right hand"* and *"holy arm"* to describe God. You might also check out the meaning of *"right hand"* (as opposed to left) in the culture of the day. You might also want to check: *What sort of literature is this?* Because if you don't ask these questions, you might run into trouble when you get to verse 8:

Let the rivers clap their hands, let the mountains sing together for joy.   **Psalm 98:8**

If you ask the question *What does it really say?*, the answer is reasonably straightforward. But if you ask the question: *What does it really mean?* – you will have to dig much deeper.

Does this verse mean that two giant hands will arise from the river and start clapping? Does it mean that the mountains will wrap their arms around each other and produce vocal chords so they can form a Choir of Hard Rocks?

If you have done your homework on *What sort of literature is this?*, the answer will not be too difficult. It is a psalm. These words are written as *poetry*. This is not an historical narrative. It is a song. It is using poetic language to illustrate a deep truth: the whole world will rejoice in the greatness of God! Even the rivers and the mountains. It is still totally true – but it is using figurative language to describe absolute truth about God.

We've now sorted out two key questions:
- What does the Bible passage really say?
- What does the Bible passage really mean?

There is now a logical third question:
- How does this Bible passage apply to us today?

We will look at that important question in the remaining sections of this book. But before we do, a very crucial prior question needs to be answered:

3. Who's in control?

This is a key question, and it is so often missed. The question is this: What is the **controlling** part of your message? That is, which part of your message will dictate the terms to the other parts?

There can be various types of biblical messages; you can have:
- **An *expository* talk** – where you unfold a continuous passage and let the Bible reveal its own message.
- **A *textual* talk** – where you simply preach on one verse, and reveal the truth it contains.
- **A *topical* talk** – where you research the Scriptures to find different verses that build a complete picture on a particular subject (eg: prayer).

a. Why expository preaching really matters

I have been teaching God's word for around thirty-five years. I have preached all these types of messages on a regular basis. My solid belief is this: the expository sermon – where you work your way through a passage and let the Bible unfold itself – is a far better teaching method than using a textual or topical Bible talk.

Especially if you get to teach God's word on a week-in-week-out basis.

While all types of Bible teaching have their merits, here are the reasons why I am convinced that continued expository preaching will develop stronger disciples than other methods:

- **It teaches people how to read the Bible:** That is, you teach from the Bible in the same way that it was written and in the same way it is meant to be read. By preaching consistently in an expository way, I am expecting that my listeners will begin reading their Bible in the same way.

- **It lets the Bible teach itself:** When you are teaching from a continuous passage, the Bible itself will dictate not only your overall message and destination, but your sub-points as well. So many times I have gone to a passage *thinking* I knew what the main point was – and discovering that as I read it, it was taking me somewhere *completely different* from what I first imagined. I have often had to change the title of my message as I let the Bible set its own destination.

- **It minimises my interference:** When I come to speak on a topic, there is the temptation for me to work out my own theology and find the verses that fit into that neatly. When I come to teach from a single text, I run the risk of steering the message according to whatever takes my fancy. That doesn't mean that I never preach topically or textually – there is a place for this from time to time. But by teaching in an expository way, it is more likely that I will let the Scriptures be my master, and I am reduced to my rightful place – a mere servant.

- **It takes us on God's journey:** By preaching through a whole book – or a whole section of a book – we get to explore the paths that God has already laid down for us. This often leads us to teach from passages that we might never have picked ourselves. By preaching in an expository way, we make sure we do not neglect the trickier parts of God's word or merely focus on our favourite texts and topics.

b. But can it be done?

If you've ever had to sit under the boring and plodding verse-by-verse sludge from an ineffective preacher – who had no engagement with you, no illustrations – and certainly no destination – you might have already decided that expository preaching is not for you. But the whole reason for this book is to help you to do it well.

You might ask: "*Is it an effective form of teaching in the twenty-first century?*"

That's a good question! Can I suggest that I answer that by referring to what I believe are the most difficult people to preach to? **Non-christian teenagers!** That's who comes to the youth group at our church. Week-in-week-out, we preach evangelistically to high-schoolers from our community. We started by opening up John's Gospel – section by section. Then in turn we worked our way through the other four Gospels. Then we started again. And here's the clincher – **we have been doing that for the last twenty years!** Yep – expository evangelistic preaching to non-Christian high-schoolers – week-in-week-out, and my experience is that it has been the most fruitful preaching we have ever done.

Go on – try it!

4. The key issue

For any message you are proclaiming, here is a key issue for you to sort out. Your message will fit into one of two categories:

- *I have my message. How can I adapt the Bible to fit into my message?* Or ...

- *I have the Bible. How can I adapt my message to fit into the Bible?*

Option One is where you start with your message – and you have to change the Bible around to fit into your message. Option Two is where you start with the Bible – and you have to adapt your message to line up with what it says. Does it make sense that only one of these leaves God in charge? Only one of these treats the Bible as God's authoritative word. And only one of these will take your passengers to a God-given destination. Option One leaves **me** in charge. Option Two leaves **God** in charge.

Here are three easy ways to get this wrong; three variations on the same theme

a. The picture-frame sermon

You know how it goes. You have a great idea for a great message. Some excellent stories. A meaty challenge. An issue you think is important. It's like a brilliant painting. The only thing you are missing is a Bible verse to put around it. You search around on your online concordance and come up with a verse that says roughly what you want it to say. Now you have your biblical frame and the whole thing masquerades as a message from the Bible.

The problem is, the Bible is meant to be the whole picture. Not just a tacky frame to adorn your man-made message. This is an example of where your wisdom and knowledge is in charge, and God's word is relegated to the position of "helpful examples".

Your message might be scintillating. Your message might be engaging. But it is a man-made message – with a biblical frame to dress it up – and it will only lead to a man-made destination.

b. The springboard sermon

Here's how this one goes: you start with a Bible verse –which sparks all sorts of ideas in your head – and the rest of your message is the exploration of all these wonderful ideas. The Bible merely acts as a springboard to launch your hearers into a pool of human wisdom. A message that is truly controlled by the Scriptures is where we all get launched into the pool of God's wisdom. God's word was never meant to be the springboard at the side of the pool. God's word is meant to be the pool itself – and the aim of your talk is that we immerse ourselves in it.

c. The appetiser sermon

I would never have believed anyone could preach like this – except I have heard it a number of times in my life. The preacher starts with a Bible verse. We all open our Bibles. The Bible text is read with great vigour and passion. Then we close our Bibles and the preacher goes on with the message that they really want to proclaim. Their message has **nothing to do with the Bible verse that started it all**.

They gave us a biblical morsel as a spiritual appetiser – and then proceeded with their *main-course sermon,* which had nothing to do with the original verse. That is not the God whom we worship. That is not trusting in God's life-giving word. God's word is not an introductory morsel. God's word is a magnificent banquet that will delight us with its abundant riches. Listen to Isaiah:

> Listen, listen to me, and eat what is good, and you will delight in the richest of fare.
> **Isaiah 55:2**

Here's the way to check whether someone is preaching an *appetiser* sermon. If you took the Bible verse out of their message, would it make any difference? If somehow you could take the Bible verse out, and you know it would not make one scrap of difference to their message – that it would stand on its own two feet – then you know it is a sermon that does not depend on the word of God.

You have now worked out what God's word is saying (Book). You know the big picture. You have your sub-points carefully worked out. You know the destination that God is taking you towards.

So, how do you get your audience to engage with you? How do you get them to decide to join you on this journey? How will you start your message?

Next Section! Read on!

Chapter 10

What is it like to live in your listeners' world?

Good question to ask.

I f you want your preaching to be effective, then you need to convey to each of your listeners that you understand something about what it is like to live in their world. You don't need to understand everything. Indeed, you can't understand everything. But all you need is one connection point. A connection that engages your listeners. A connection that makes them feel *This person at the front giving this message – they understand what I'm going through.*

How you start your message – what you use for your Hook - really matters!

There are three key questions to ask to help you have a riveting and effective hook. Here they are:

1.   **What's it like to live in your listeners' world?**
2.   **Why would they want to go to your destination?**
3.   **Why would they engage with YOU?**

We will spend one chapter on each of these questions. Let's tackle the first one:

What's it like to live in your listeners' world?

A good teacher knows the importance of correctly interpreting the text. But you also need to **correctly interpret the congregation**.

If you do not get inside the mind of your hearers, you might well miss the mark in delivering your message.

I was at a church once where the congregation included a large number of local teenagers. They were mostly from non-Christian homes, and most of them had little idea of what following Jesus really meant. Indeed, many of them had not yet arrived at the point where they were prepared to commit their life to following Jesus.

We had a new minister arrive who didn't take the time to get to know his people. He was preaching a series through the commandments, and he had arrived at this commandment: *"Honour your father and your mother"*. He remarked to the congregation: *"Of course we all want to obey our mum and dad, don't we?"* The young people just looked at each other. I could tell by the looks on their faces that they were mouthing the words: *"No, we don't"*. And because they perceived that the speaker didn't understand them at all, **they switched off immediately.** They were no longer engaged.

I was once invited to speak at a prestigious boys' school; one where the overwhelming majority of students were boarders. They lived at the school throughout the school term, and only went home to their families during the holiday breaks.

I had absolutely no idea of what it is like to live that way. I have never experienced anything in my life that comes close. I knew that if I were to understand their world, I would need to do some hard work. I tracked down a few boys from that school who attended my church – I spent about half an hour with them listening and asking questions – and I gained enough insight to understand the world of the boarders to whom I was going to speak later that week.

You get to understand your hearers by asking a series of questions. This might seem like a long list, but remember, you might only use one of these references in your Hook. You only need one connection point to communicate that you understand something of their world.

You will discover some biblical examples of this in Chapter 14.

Play around with these questions:

a. What current events is everyone talking about?

Stay up to date with the world your audience lives in. If they live in your own community, and they are about your age, and come from the same cultural background, you might have an idea of what issues are relevant without asking too many questions. But as soon as you have to teach a group that contains people from a different age-group, or who live in a different location, or who have a different cultural background – you have some work to do.

If you travel to another city to talk, then ask the cab driver what everyone is talking about. What's the latest political scandal? What sporting event is coming up? What big, new project is under way? What's everyone complaining about? If you can get a quick idea of what is topical, then you have a good chance of engaging your audience.

What would you do if you had to speak to a group who were in their first year of high school? The things they are talking about might be very different from the issues you are aware of! The best way to find out? Ask them! Hang around with a few of them. Listen to what they say. Ask them what they mean.

b. What do they laugh at?

Everybody loves to laugh, but not everybody laughs at the same thing. Spend some time with the people you will be speaking to and observe what they laugh at. If you say something in your sermon that you think is outrageously funny, but you only get a polite titter in response – it might not be that your line wasn't funny. It might just be that it wasn't funny to these people.

I fell into this trap once. We have two youth groups at our church – one for senior high, and one for junior high. I was invited to teach the same message at each group. I designed the message with the older group in mind, and imagined I could just make it a bit simpler for the younger group.

But in the younger group, my humour bombed! I had a number of very clever and witty remarks that made the senior highs roar with laughter. But at the junior-high group, they just sat there with bemused looks on their faces. *They laughed at different things!* Junior highs don't go for clever witty humour. They love slapstick! Tell a story about your pants falling down, or getting a cream pie thrown in your face. That's what they laugh at.

c. What do they make jokes about?

Listen to the jokes that your intended audience will tell each other. What off-hand comical references do they make? Who is the butt of all their jokes?

Is there a politician or other public figure who is routinely laughed at? Is there a government policy that everyone treats as a joke? Is there a bottom-placed sports team that is struggling to get a win? While we don't want to reinforce the prejudices that people might have, an *occasional* or *slight* reference to a popular target will help people to feel: *I think the preacher understands my world.*

d. What do they think is "cool"?

In every culture, there are some things that are really prized and valued. Things that everyone wants to have. The latest craze. The latest fad. If you work with young people, you will know that these fads change extremely rapidly. Don't get caught out with an out-of-date term! Once again, simply observe them interacting with each other. Find out what they value.

For teenagers it might be a clothing brand or an electronic gizmo. For young marrieds it might be the latest baby buggy with go-anywhere-wheels and the inbuilt Blu-ray player for little bubsy. For older folk, it might be their grandchildren.

What music is *in*? What music or fashion is definitely *out*? See if you can find out what is highly prized. This will be very useful in your illustrations.

e. What do they complain about?

This will produce gold for you! In every group there is something that everyone is moaning about. A government project. The traffic. Too much homework. Slow internet. Listen carefully – it won't take you long to spot what your listeners are sick of.

f. What are they hoping for?

What would they love to achieve? What would they like to happen right now? For the mortgage to be paid off? For school holidays? For the next job promotion? A new car? Peace in their family? A moment of quietness to rest? More money? Someone to really love them? If you can identify with people's hopes – you will have strong engagement with them.

g. What do they get wrong?

What are the particular sins of your audience? Where have they lost the plot? Where do they need extra encouragement? If they're going to do something that is wrong, what are they likely to do? What temptations do they struggle with? What pressures are they facing?

When I spoke at that prestigious boys' school, I asked a few of the students: *"If you wanted to sneak off and do something wrong at school, what would you do? What's the thing that everyone talks about 'getting away with'?"* Their answer? *"Smoking in the durrie-holes"*. Now I hadn't heard the word durrie for some time. It is an Aussie slang word for cigarette. The durrie-holes were apparently holes in the school hedge where you could hide and have a smoke without getting caught. I simply slipped that into one of my early sentences when I addressed the whole school. They were instantly engaged!

Where the two worlds intersect

Here are the two worlds that you need to understand. The first one is to understand God's Word.

God's word
What the Bible says

The Book
The Look
The Took
Your destination

The second world you need to understand is **Their World.** That is – what world do your listeners live in? What is their life really like?

Their world
The world your listeners live in

The Hook

Your starting point

Their world	H	God's word
The world your listeners live in	**O**	**What the Bible says**
	O	
The Hook	**K**	*The Book*
		The Look
		The Took
Your starting point		*Your destination*

Now here's the key question: **Where do the two worlds intersect?** That is, from the point of view of someone living in your listener's world, where is there already a common point in something to do with your destination? Because where the two worlds overlap, **that's where you start your hook.**

I was to present a message on "God's justice" to high-schoolers. So the question to ask was: *In their world, where are they already personally aware of the issue of justice and injustice?* The two answers I immediately came up with were:

- when a parent or teacher accuses them unfairly – and they get in trouble when in fact they have done nothing wrong.
- when some bigger kid pushes in front of them at the school lunch room.

That's where the two worlds intersect!

This will give you the clue as to where to start your Hook. Here are some possible starting lines to engage high-schoolers on the topic of "justice":

- *Have you ever had a teacher get you in trouble – when in fact you have done nothing wrong at all?*

- *What does it feel like when some kid who is bigger than you pushes in front of you in the school food line?*
- *When I was at school, I had this teacher who was always picking on me. Whenever anything went wrong – it was always me who got the blame. It was so unfair.*

If you can start your Hook where the two worlds intersect – you will get an instant connection. Your audience is now engaged.

So the first question to ask to engage your audience right at the start... the first thing to check if you want to attract attention with your opening line... the key factor to coming up with a compelling and powerful hook... is...

What is it like to live in your listeners' world?

Chapter 11

Why would they want to go to your destination?

One of the biggest dangers in preaching – one of the main reasons that Bible teachers fail to engage their listeners – is this: **the preacher assumes that their listeners *want* to go to the same destination as them.** They think that by simply announcing their topic – or reading their Bible text – or even by opening the scriptures – their congregation will be salivating at the mouth with excitement – thrilled beyond measure to be taken to the wonderful destination that has been announced by the hard-working and faithful preacher.

In my experience, the above scenario does not take into account the doctrine of sin. We are all sinful people – and every part of us is pervaded by sin. Even our thought patterns, as the preacher ascends the dais for *yet another sermon,* are corrupted by sin.

My experience as a Bible teacher has taught me that very few people in the audience initially want to go to the same destination as me. You might think that my outlook is a little negative. Or that maybe I preach to very sinful congregations. Or perhaps it's because I'm a youth pastor!

But it is also *my own* experience. I suspect I have heard enough sermons to last me a number of lifetimes. So sometimes when I am sitting there at church, and it's time for the sermon – my heart is not always racing with excitement because I know God's word is about to be opened. I am not always interested in what the speaker has to say. I sometimes don't care a lot about their topic. On occasions I don't particularly want to go to their destination. I am easily distracted. Maybe it's because I'm tired. Perhaps it's because I've had a hard day. Maybe I'm just old and grouchy. Or it might just be that I really am extremely sinful.

But when I walk up to the front to open God's word to a congregation, my starting assumption is: *Hardly anyone here probably wants to go to this destination with me*. It is that starting assumption that has led me to work very hard at those opening few minutes when I get started with my Hook.

Am I the only one who feels disengaged sometimes? C'mon – you have sat there – at least some of the time – when someone has been proclaiming the living word of God – and you have been totally *disengaged*. Admit it. It happens. Even with the best of intentions, it is so easy to simply tune-out.

If you've put a lot of work into your message; if you've laboured long hours to carefully understand and explain the passage; if you've included some great stories to illustrate your points; if you've carefully worked out a great destination with a powerful challenge at the end – you don't want to go on this amazing journey **and leave all your potential passengers at the station!**

So ask the question: *Why would my listeners **want** to travel to my destination with me?* And if your answer is: *Because it's true* or *Because it's God's Word* – you have missed the point. Because you know that you haven't always been interested in a sermon that is being preached to you – just because it's true – just because it's God's word. Right?

We need to offer some motivation for the listener to, in fact, *listen*. If the Bible passage is going to provide a great answer – we need to help the listener work out *What is the question?* If we're going to provide a solution from God's word, then we need to help the listener work out *What is the problem?* If we are going to reveal something from the Scriptures that we are convinced our listeners need to hear, we ought to help them work out *Why do I need to hear this?* That is the skill of a preacher. To engage an audience so that they want to hear what God says about their situation.

Here are four key questions to help you sort it through:

1. What are they already thinking about my destination?

If you're a guest speaker at the Stamp Collectors' Club – and your topic is *Why I love stamps* – then your audience might already be interested in your destination. If you're talking to young mums, and your title is *How to develop your baby in the first 12 months*, then you could assume they are onside from the very start.

If you're speaking to teenagers, and your topic is *Let's talk about sex* – I suspect you will have their interest. But they might not agree with your destination! If your basic destination is to say: *God made sex to be beautiful, but we have trashed it by moving outside his guidelines* then you need to ask yourself: *What are these teenagers already thinking about the topic of sex before I start?* And if they're a regular bunch of church-going teenagers, they might be thinking: *I thought sex was bad. But the best way to have fun is to use it any way you want. But God doesn't want us to enjoy it. He's put all sorts of restrictions on it – which I resent. And I don't want to hear from the Bible. It will just make me feel more guilty.*

If that is what they're really thinking, then they might not want to go to your destination at all. If people know that your destination might challenge them to a higher level of discipleship and accountability, they might be reluctant to go there. If your listeners know that your destination is going to call them to repentance, they might never want to engage with you on your journey.

That's why you need to ask the question: *What are they already thinking about my destination?* Because you might work out:

- that they passionately agree with your destination, *or*

- that they agree with your destination – but don't really want to put it into action, *or*
- that they passionately **disagree** with your destination and will fight you every step of the way.

Depending on the stance they are taking, your Hook might need to be very different.

The place where I noticed this most acutely was when teaching Scripture at the local state high school. In Australia, Scripture (the technical name is Special Religious Education) is the opportunity for Christians to go into their local public schools to teach religion to those students of the same faith. In general terms, there are a lot of students whose parents have nominated a Christian denomination for their child – without their child having any real faith or interest in Jesus. Walking into a classroom in a public high school and announcing: *"I'm here to teach you about Jesus"* would no doubt be met by a tsunami of indifference and hostility.

So the question I had to ask every time I entered a classroom to teach Scripture was: *What are they already thinking about my destination?* Invariably, the answers I came up with were:

- *This is going to be boring.*
- *I don't want to be here.*
- *I don't think it's true anyway.*
- *Even if it's true, it is not relevant to me.*

Does it make sense that if your Hook does not disarm these defences, then you will *never* engage these students on a journey that will take them to Jesus?

This is easy to see when entering the hostile territory of a Scripture classroom. But here's where the danger comes when teaching the Bible in a church context. Once you're back in the safety of your own church service – "preaching to the converted" – the temptation is to think: *Now we're back on home turf – everyone is onside with where I want to head in my message.*

I have three words to say. *No, they're not!*

They might look as if they're on board. They might sound as if they're on board. And maybe some of them are. But if you assume everyone's on board, you run the risk of driving an empty train to your wonderful destination – and that means – nobody gets anywhere.

The first key question to ask when working out your Hook is: *What are they already thinking about my destination?* Your answer needs to be brutally honest.

2. What is their resistance level?

Any message from God which calls people to a high level of discipleship will usually hit a resistance level in your hearers. They might not want to hear what God has to say on a certain topic; or maybe they already know what you will say is true, but deep down they don't want to do it. The higher your challenge, the higher their resistance will be.

You need to work out: *Where in their life are they failing to put this into action? Where have they settled for a second-best option? What are the excuses they offer for not obeying in this area?*

If you are preaching to people that God has first call on their finances; if you are calling on teenagers to honour and respect their parents; if you are challenging Christians to obey the law by keeping the speed limit and being scrupulously honest with their taxes; if you are calling single young adults to sexual purity; if you are challenging non-Christians to surrender their whole life to Jesus – **then you can expect that the resistance levels will be high.**

If you don't work out what the various resistances are in your listeners, then it is unlikely that you will be able to break through their resistance, and equally unlikely that you will engage them to take this journey with you.

3. Can I get them to agree to the concept in their everyday life?

There will be spiritual concepts that will be hard to understand, and biblical commands that are difficult to obey. Early on in my preparation, I want to see whether I can help my listeners to see that the principle I am about to teach is a good principle – and something which they are already doing in their everyday life.

For example, if I want to teach the biblical value of sacrificing my whole life to Jesus, then I need to anticipate what the resistance levels might be. Quite possibly, most people don't like the idea of surrender or sacrifice. They would think that it means giving in to someone else – where the other person becomes the winner and they themselves become the loser. They would think that giving something up would mean their life would be less enjoyable. It is distinctly possible they would resist my message on sacrifice and surrender.

So here's the question I want to ask: *Where is this principle of sacrifice or surrender already well accepted in their everyday life?*

Every time they buy something they are sacrificing their money because they believe that what they spend their money on will make their life better. University and college students spend endless hours waiting on tables and doing other menial jobs because they know they need to do this to finance their education. Parents will make extraordinary sacrifices for the sake of their children. I want to help people to agree that they are already committed to the idea of sacrifice. That is, they will gladly surrender their own money, time and energies where they believe that what they gain far outweighs what they lose.

Once people have accepted their own willingness to sacrifice things in their everyday life, then their resistance level to surrendering everything to Jesus has been substantially lessened.

Work out your listeners' resistance levels early in your preparation, because this will be a key part to your Hook.

4. If we're providing the solution, what is the problem?

If God's word is supplying the answer, then what is the question? And why should I worry about the solution if I can't see there is a problem in my life?

Most people don't want to listen to anything unless it is offering them something that they really want. And most people don't know that they want it unless they are aware that they have a problem without it. This is a sad statement, but it is true. It is an example of how sin has pervaded every area of our lives.

If you want people to enthusiastically embrace God's solution, then they need to feel the pain of the problem. If you want people to willingly search for God's answer, then they need to feel the depth of this unanswered question in their life. Until they realise their own need, they might not be interested at all in your wonderful destination.

Our church was preaching through the Apostles' Creed. The senior pastor had opened the series with *"I believe in God"*. I was handed the second message: *"the Father almighty, creator of heaven and earth"*. I was preaching in a community where there was a lot of hurt. There were stacks of young people in our church who had fairly abysmal family lives. My destination was to take them to the God who is *"Father"*, *"Almighty"* and *"Creator"*.

My suspicion was that they believed these three things already. They agreed with the doctrine. But my further suspicion was that there was an emotional blockage to treating God as *"Father"*. Their own experience with their own dads was often fragile and painful. Added to that, their experience with anyone in authority – anyone with power – was one of rebellion and bitterness. If their own dads had mistreated them, imagine submitting to a heavenly Father who had *unlimited power* and could do anything He wanted!

In one sense, I had answered the question: *What are they already thinking about my destination?* But now I needed to tackle a further question: *If we're providing the solution, what is the problem?* My Hook was to talk about the problems we had with our own dads.

The pain that had been caused by their neglect. The longing we all had to be loved by a dad and accepted no matter what. I don't think most people were ready to get on board with my destination of an *all-powerful Father* until they had felt the pain of what it is like never to be loved that way.

This has implications for when we preach evangelistically. Let's imagine that in your audience there are a number of unsaved and nominal believers. A number of guests have been invited. There are quite a few first-timers present. If our aim is to help people trust their whole life to the saving power of the Christ who died and rose for them – then that clearly is our destination.

But ask the question: *Why would any non-Christian want to go to that destination?* If I just stand up and announce *You need Jesus*, their most likely response will be: *"No I don't. I'm living a comfortable life. I have almost everything I need. I'm happy for other people to believe in Jesus – but I don't need him"*. That answers the question: *What are they already thinking about my destination?*

So if we ask a further question: **If we're providing the solution, what is the problem?** this might be a harder one to answer. The problem might be crystal clear to us. But our potential passengers are probably already thinking: *I don't have a problem.* Biblically, we know that the reason they do not think they need Jesus is that they do not realise the enormity of His sacrifice and rescue through his death and resurrection. The reason they do not understand this is that they do not realise the enormity and ugliness of their own sin. The reason they do not understand this is that they do not understand the absolute holiness and purity of God. That is, God hates sin so much that no-one with any sin in them can ever approach him. That's why we need Jesus!

So – where do you start? How do you engage them? This requires you to carefully get inside the minds of your hearers. Do you engage them on understanding the holiness of God? Do you engage them on understanding the enormity of their sin? Do you engage them on the hopelessness of searching for alternatives other than Jesus? There is no one-size-fits-all answer to this question – but the very fact that you are asking these questions and searching for a point of engagement means it is highly likely that you will do a better job of engaging your listeners than if you had never asked the questions.

In a recent camp for our young people, I presented an evangelistic message. They were a reasonably church-oriented bunch, but there was a number of attenders who were fairly nominal, and just coming along because their friends were there. I desperately wanted to bring them to Christ. How would I engage them so they wanted to take the journey to Christ with me?

I was teaching the Bible from Mark 10:17-34 – The rich young ruler. Here was the description of a man who was getting all the activities right, but yet his heart was not fully surrendered to Jesus. I wanted my listeners to understand that truth about him. That was my destination. That's where I wanted to take everyone.

I worked through the steps to help answer the question: *Why would they want to go to my destination?* Step one was to ask: *What are they already thinking about my destination?* Because I knew these young people fairly well, I suspected that they were feeling: *I believe all this stuff about Jesus. But I don't want to commit myself to him. My life is going okay. But sometimes it feels a bit pointless.*

That also answered my next question: *If we're offering the solution, what is the problem?* That's where I started my Hook. We talked about doing things that feel pointless. Putting in the bare minimum of effort because you can't see any real purpose in it. We had some funny stories about jobs they hate doing; boring family reunions; subjects at school which don't seem to have a point; relationships that have gone stale. They started to feel the emptiness of doing things at the surface level, but not having your heart engaged. It was a short step to then ask: *"Does your Christianity feel like that sometimes?"* That took us straight to the rich young ruler – a man who did all the activities of his faith, but his heart was not in it.

Don't just announce your destination and hope that people want to hop on board. Before you prepare your journey, ask this key question: *Why would your listeners want to go to your destination?* Until you can work out the answer to that question, I don't think you will take anyone on a journey that day.

Chapter 12

Why would your listeners engage with YOU?

There are three key questions we are dealing with to help you get all your passengers on board before you start your journey:

- **Chapter 10 – What is it like to live in your listeners' world?** This question tackles your intentional engagement with your listeners and their world. If you do not understand the world of your listeners, you have little hope of engaging them on any journey.

- **Chapter 11 – Why would they want to go to your destination?** This question tackles your listeners' engagement with your destination. If your listeners have no interest in your destination, they will never journey with you.

In this chapter we wrestle with the third key question: **Why would your listeners want to engage with YOU?** If your listeners do not sense an engagement and connection with you, the preacher; if they do not learn to trust you as a train-driver – then they won't let you take them anywhere.

Have you worked out that the key word is engagement? This is vital throughout your whole message, but especially so at the beginning. If you do not engage your listeners with your opening Hook, then they will never even start the journey with you.

So, how do you help your listeners to trust you and engage with you? Here are some guidelines that I have found helpful. Not every preacher has to slavishly follow these "rules". In fact, often I vary them myself. But if you're looking to engage your audience with you, here are some guidelines that will really help you:

1. Engage them with your first sentence

Not your second sentence. Not your tenth sentence. Your first sentence. Because in your first sentence, they will decide whether to listen to your second sentence. If you lose them right at the start, it is very hard to win them back.

You know what it's like. You're sitting in a waiting room somewhere, leafing through a magazine. You look at the first article. You flip the page and look at the second article. You keep doing this until you find an article that you want to read. Then you get stuck into reading the story that interests you.

Let's analyse what just went on. How did you decide which article to read? How did you make the decision as to whether to flip the page or get engrossed? Here's what probably happened:

- You looked at the headline or photo to see whether it interested you.
- If it was of some vague interest, you read the first sentence.
- If the first sentence didn't grab you, you turned the page.

There might have been fascinating stuff buried somewhere on page 2, but if the first sentence didn't grab you, you never read any further. Somewhere in that first sentence (or, if you're very gracious, the first paragraph) you determined whether you were engaged enough to read any further.

It's exactly the same when someone is preaching. Somewhere in your first sentence people decide whether your second sentence is worth listening to. If your opening line doesn't arrest their attention, you will have to work overtime to get it back.

Here are some suggestions to engage people with your first sentence:

a. Write it down and stick to it

You might have flexibility in every other point of your message, but once you have worked out your opening line – stick to it no matter what. You might do the rest of your notes in bullet-point form – but write out your opening line in full.

If you think of a funny idea as you walk to the platform; if you trip on the microphone cable on the way up; if you suddenly recognise a face in the crowd – ignore all this and stick to your opening line. You have put time and thought into this. This is the line that will get passengers off the platform and onto your train. Invariably, the spontaneous thought that you have at the last moment will not be nearly as effective.

b. Engage the listeners' imagination ... and

c. Describe an everyday occurrence they can identify with

We'll run these two together. Can you ask a question that sparks the listeners' imagination by describing a situation that they can easily identify with? This sort of question will engage the listeners' creativity as they start to work out their own individual answer. Can you start a thought process in their minds that will have them picturing their own response? Can you start a chain of events that most people could easily identify with?

Have you ever had one of those days where everything seems to go wrong?

This sort of question engages the listeners on two levels. On one hand, they start to recall a day in their own life where everything did seem to go wrong. They can identify with it – and they start to picture it in their mind. But secondly, their expectation is primed that you are about to tell them a funny example of where things did go wrong for you. People love to laugh at the misfortunes of others – and so the expectation that you will tell of your mishaps is an incentive to keep listening.

There are many variations on this theme:

You know what I hate? I hate waiting in line...

We set out for our family holiday. Everything was going to be perfect. Little did we realise what was around the corner ...

I remember my first kiss ...

When I was at school, there was a day that I dreaded more than any other ...

Can your opening line engage your listener's imagination by describing an event they can easily identify with?

d. Head towards your destination
Whatever you decide is going to be your opening line, ask this key question: *Does this take us towards our destination, or is it a distraction from our destination?* The best opening lines engage the listeners on the actual journey. They are the first steps towards the destination. The ideal Hook raises a question that will be answered in your Took.

e. Use observational humour
We will say more about humour later in this book, but wise use of humour can be one of the most effective weapons to penetrate people's defences. When people are laughing, their guard is down. When people are laughing, they are being drawn closer to you.

When people are laughing, they will accept an insightful challenge that they might otherwise reject in a more serious moment.

You will note that I suggested observational humour. That is, can you describe a normal, everyday event – and show the funny or ridiculous side of it? For some people this will come naturally. Others of you will think: *I'm not a very funny person*. But wherever you sit on the humour spectrum, you can learn to be better at it.

Are there some preachers you listen to who are naturally funny? Are there some professional comedians whose work you admire? You can learn a lot by watching the professionals at work. My two favourite observational comedians are Carl Barron and Jimeoin. They don't tell jokes. They don't have punch lines. They simply observe everyday life and show the funny side of it. Grab one of their DVDs or look them up on YouTube and learn from their style.

If you're not sure that what you say will be funny, try it on some trusted friends who will be brutally honest with you. If, after many attempts, you conclude that you are not yet good enough with humour to use it, then don't use it yet. Using no humour is better than using bad humour! If you need some help with humour, check out chapters 22 and 23 later in this book.

This doesn't mean you should start with a joke. This can be very dangerous. You'll see why below!

Dangerous opening lines

BEWARE!! Use any of the following at your own peril! Most of these are guaranteed to derail your passengers even before the journey starts!

Some of the seasoned professionals can get away with these openers. But that is due to the skill they have refined over many decades. If you are still developing your preaching, most of the following lines are way too risky.

a. Don't start with a joke

I know I said: "Use observational humour", but don't start with a joke. A joke is an artificial setup – with a punch line at the end. *There was an Englishmen, an Irishman and a Scotsman who walked into a bar …*

Why not start with a joke? Because…

- Most jokes are really not very funny. Seriously, most are not worth telling. Most jokes produce a groan rather than a laugh.
- What if it falls flat? If your joke doesn't work, your whole journey is potentially derailed.
- Unless you're a seasoned pro, opening with a joke is just way too risky.

b. Don't start with a movie clip

I know it will arrest people's attention if you start with a movie clip. And it is kind of creative. But here's what I've found nearly all the time: the audience thinks that the movie clip is more interesting than listening to me! That is, when the movie clip finishes, and I start my message, you can almost hear an audible groan. People are disappointed – they wanted to see more of the movie. I don't want to start my message with people feeling disappointed!

c. Don't use shock tactics

I want to talk to you about sex! Good! Now that I've got your attention, let me turn to my real topic of the Immanence and Transcendence of God.

Okay – you got their attention, but at what cost? You've almost admitted that you couldn't get their attention with your actual topic – so you have set them up to think it's boring. And you have now eaten away at your integrity. People don't like being tricked into listening. They will tend to disregard any emphatic thing you say from this point.

d. Don't tell disconnected stories

I have heard this technique used by many Bible teachers. They open their message with a funny story that has nothing to do with their subject. Once people have stopped laughing, then they get on with their real topic. It seems that the point of the opening joke is to *"warm the crowd up"* – and having achieved that, they then head off on their real journey.

An ideal Hook will directly connect with where the journey is heading. The Hook is an integral part of the journey; it is the first step towards the destination. Telling a disconnected joke is like luring people onto your train with a carnival sideshow, and once they're on board, you sneakily leave the station without announcing your destination. Don't do it! Long term, it will lower your integrity and work against you.

e. "Does this mic work?" (tap... tap)

You just lost your audience. Maybe you need to know if the mic works, but they don't. Trust the audio team. And if your mic doesn't work, then start again – with a different mic – or just a very loud voice. You might feel embarrassed, but your audience doesn't.

f. "I'm not very good at public speaking..."

If this is true, it will become painfully obvious in the next few minutes. No need to tell us.

Bottom line? Don't start with an apology.

"I've had a really busy week, and I haven't had as much time to prepare as normal..." This might matter to you, but it doesn't matter to your audience. Just start. Your audience will never know the difference.

Don't start with an apology. All you will do is lower the expectations – and lower the result. Starting with an apology is very unprofessional. If life has been difficult in your run-up to this message, then charge ahead anyway and trust God for the results.

g. Don't just announce your topic

- *Open your Bibles at…*
- *My text for today is…*
- *I want to tell you about (pick your topic, subject or destination)…*

When you say predictable things like this right at the start, your audience take the first step towards disengaging with you.

Okay – Step One was to engage your listeners with your opening sentence. Now we move to Step Two:

2. Establish an emotional connection in the first few minutes

Here's what I mean by an emotional connection – that your listeners will be nodding their heads, agreeing with you and saying to themselves: *This preacher understands what I'm going through.* Of course, you won't understand exactly what every member of the audience is going through. But as you engage people on your journey, you can let them know, in general terms, that you understand the world in which they live. That you have struggles just like they do.

I was doing a recent sermon on *"The Power of Words"* from Ephesians 4. **My opening line was**: *"Sticks and stones may break my bones, but words can never hurt me. True or false?"* I then gave everyone thirty seconds to discuss their answer with the person next to them. The words I quoted are a popular children's rhyme, and I wanted to arrest people's attention by intriguing them as to whether this popular rhyme was true or false.

But I then went on to make an **emotional connection**. That is, to say things that would probably ring true in the experience of my listeners. I said things like:

"You know that old 'Sticks and stones' rhyme is false because you know you've been hurt by someone else's words. Maybe you

did something and nobody thanked you. Perhaps you had an idea and someone else said it was stupid. Maybe you tried really hard, but you were simply told you were not good enough. At some stage, every one of us has felt put down by someone else's words."

My intention in saying this was to make an emotional connection with my audience. I wanted them to be nodding their heads, saying: *"This preacher understands my life"*. I wanted them to engage with me so that I could take them on the rest of the journey.

I could have presented the same information another way. I could have quoted statistics which show that 92% of all people have felt significant hurt because they have been put down by the words of others. I could have said: *"Words are powerful because God's word says so"*. But by making the emotional connection, I wanted to engage people's thought process, so that they could work out for themselves:

- *This guy is describing my life.*
- *I know words are powerful because I've been hurt by them.*
- *I now want to learn more about how to use words in a more positive way.*

That's an emotional connection. Where possible, I want to make an emotional connection with my listeners somewhere in the opening few minutes, so that they are engaged for the journey and wanting to discover the destination that God's word will take them to.

This emotional engagement is your listeners' **buy-in**. That is, when you have engaged them emotionally, they have bought in to your journey. Your opening line might arrest their attention; your stories might be quite interesting – but unless your listeners buy in to your journey – then you will not be taking them anywhere with your message that day.

This buy-in really matters. As I look back at my messages that I preached when I was much less experienced, I have discovered to my horror that I usually left this step out. Indeed, as a Bible teacher, you want a few different buy-ins in the early stages of your message. More about this in the next chapter!

As I listen to other preachers, and coach them in their craft, *this is the step that is most often left out.* That is, they will have an arresting and engaging opening, which is quickly followed by moving straight to their topic. There is no emotional engagement.

As a Bible teacher, you need to keep asking yourself these questions: *Why would any of my listeners want to travel to my destination? What need can I connect with in their life that will make them search for this answer with me?* And here is the reason why you need to ask these questions: because your listeners will be asking those questions themselves! There is a resistance point you need to overcome. The resistance point is: *Why should I listen to you? What have you got to teach me? Why should I care about your destination?*

Sure – I know some people will be godly enough to think: *This is God's word. Of course I'm interested in listening.* But experience has taught me that these people are in the minority. Whenever I am preaching, I want to ask: *How do I connect with the person who is uninterested and disengaged? How can I tap into something within them that will motivate them to get on board and start exploring the destination with me?* That's the emotional connection I am talking about.

A young colleague of mine is a brilliant preacher. First rate. Always engaging. Always interesting. He started a recent sermon by swinging a cricket bat, and told us some funny stories about his cricket days as a boy. Then he picked up a baseball bat, and explained that he had now started playing a completely different game. Because he was playing a whole different ball game, he had to re-learn how to use a bat. Very funny stuff. Very well explained.

Then he went to Acts 17 and explained that Paul in Athens was facing a completely different ball game. These people were unlike others he had encountered, so he needed to minister to them in a different way. My colleague concluded that modern life in Australia was like Athens – we were reaching out to people who didn't have a basic faith structure behind them. He then went on to explain how Paul went about ministering to those in Athens. This gave us clues as to how we minister to those around us.

A great message. **But the bit he missed out was the emotional connection.** There was nothing in what he said that motivated me to explore his destination. I found it amusing that he had to change his batting style when he moved from cricket to baseball, and I found it interesting that Paul had to change his ministry style when he went to Athens, but there was nothing in his introduction that tapped into my emotions to cause me to think: *Hang on – that's* ***me*** *he's talking about. That keeps happening in my life. I wonder what the answer is?*

How could he have achieved this emotional connection? Simply by inserting a few lines between his baseball story and his Acts 17 story. Something like:

Maybe you've found yourself in a new situation where you realised it was a whole different ball game. Perhaps you've started in a brand new school or college – and everything is done in a completely different way. Maybe you've been in a long-standing relationship which hasn't worked out – and you're not sure of which way to turn. Perhaps you've grown up with a strong Christian community around you, but now that you've started your first full-time job – you realise that the people around you don't share your Christian faith – and you're not quite sure how to approach them. Wouldn't it be great to learn how to deal with this new situation? Come with me to Acts 17..."

That's the emotional connection. If you bypass it, you make it harder for your listeners to engage with your journey.

Let's check: how do you help your listeners to engage with you?

1. **Engage them with your first sentence.**
2. **Establish an emotional connection in the first few minutes.**

And now for Step Three:

3. Earn their trust by being trustworthy

It's not just fine words that will move an audience. Your listeners need to see that you have a solid character that is backing up your words. They need to know that you are a person of authenticity and integrity. They need to see that you practise what you preach.

The Bible puts it this way:

> In everything set them an example by doing what is good. In your teaching show integrity, seriousness and soundness of speech that cannot be condemned, so that those who oppose you may be ashamed because they have nothing bad to say about us.
> **Titus 2:7-8**

"In your teaching show integrity." Words worth remembering.

Yes, you need to get your words right. You need to carefully unpack the Bible so that people can see clearly what God is saying to them from the Scriptures. And you need to do it with passion – not in a dry and disinterested way. But most importantly, people need to see it is coming from a Bible teacher whose life has been fashioned by the very words they are proclaiming. If there is even a hint that the preacher is pretending, or mouthing meaningless words, your listeners will never trust you enough to take them to your destination.

One of the advantages of being a week-in-week-out preacher

with the same congregation is that your listeners get to know you – your failings and your triumphs – and you start to teach them with the voice of authenticity. It has to come from the heart. You can't fake integrity – well, not for very long, anyway. If you want your listeners to trust you, you must keep showing them that you're trustworthy.

Here are some guidelines which will help:

a. Be trustworthy with the Scriptures
As you keep handling the Scriptures in a genuine and submissive way, people will start to trust you to take them on a journey.

> Do your best to present yourself to God as one approved, a worker who does not need to be ashamed and who correctly handles the word of truth.   **2 Timothy 2:15**

b. Be pastoral in your approach
I worked alongside a colleague once. He was a fine preacher. And yet most people in church thought he was angry. That was the style he had. That's what came across to most people. He was not pastoral in his approach from the pulpit. People became reluctant to let him take them on a journey.

When you are preaching in public, you are pastoring in public. You are not speaking to a crowd – or even to a congregation. You are speaking to individuals who have real needs and real hurts. This pastoral understanding you have has to be communicated by the words that you use, and the approach that you have.

c. Be transparent in what you say
You need to reveal that you are a fellow struggler with your listeners. That you face the same trials and temptations as they do. That you experience the same successes and failures that they

experience. That you are not the grand master who has already arrived at the destination, but that you are a fellow traveller in their journey through life.

Don't make yourself the hero in all your stories. Tell some stories about your failures. Let them know about your struggles. Confess to them where you have fallen. As you reveal yourself in this transparent way, your listeners will be encouraged to journey with you, and to trust you to take them to your destination.

So – how do you actually prepare an opening Hook so that you engage your listeners on your journey?

Read on!

Chapter 13

Engaging your audience – one step at a time

The whole purpose of the Hook is to engage each of your listeners so they might want to take this journey with you. Of course, you could just announce the destination – and you would get the people who are already interested. *"I want to speak to you about world religions"*.

If you simply started like this, you would engage all the people who were interested in world religions, and disengage all those who had no interest at all. The whole purpose of the Hook is to engage people **who might never have thought about your destination.** *You* know it's important for them to go there; *they* haven't yet realised it. The Hook is a way of helping people to realise the value of your destination – one step at a time.

There's a deliberate flow in a good opening to any message. You start at a fairly general level where it is easy for people to agree with you – and with every step you take them a little deeper. At the beginning of your message, many will have no idea as to why they should get on board your train and travel with you. The effective Bible teacher will help people to engage at the general level, and then progressively engage them at a deeper level as the journey continues.

We've already looked at the three key questions you need to ask to engage your listeners so they will want to go on your journey with you:

1.   **What's it like to live in your listeners' world?**
2.   **Why would they want to go to your destination?**
3.   **Why would they engage with YOU?**

Here now are the four key steps as to how the beginning of your message will lead your listeners to a deeper and deeper engagement – one step at a time:

1.   **Arrest their attention**
2.   **Secure their agreement**
3.   **Deepen their engagement**
4.   **Intensify their desire**

Let's check these out.

1. Arrest their attention

How will you grab your audience's attention with your first sentence? We have already looked at this in detail in Chapter 12. This step will engage your listeners at a fairly general – and dare I say it – superficial level. That's why your next step needs to engage them one level deeper.

2. Secure their agreement

How can you get your listeners to agree with the general principle you are proposing? Whatever your destination, whatever your point of challenge – can you get your listeners to agree to this by showing them how they are already committed to this principle in their everyday life?

This is your first *buy-in* point. And you will aim to deepen their buy-in at each of the subsequent levels.

This is an important step. If you can get your listeners to agree with your principle in an easy-going everyday situation, then it is not a hard job to get them to agree with the same principle in a more serious or challenging aspect of their life. That's why it's important that your next step takes them to a deeper level.

3. Deepen their engagement

How do you help your listeners to take your message to heart on a deeper level? How do you get them to agree that there might be an area of their life that they need to change? How do you inspire their engagement so that they are willing to be challenged on a personal level?

Here's a helpful flow that will get you there:

a. The light-hearted level

Can you describe an everyday situation – maybe even a humorous situation – where it is very easy for your listeners to agree with you because it is light-hearted and there are no serious consequences? Sometimes this might be a funny story, but it does not need to be. But it does need to be a story that relates to the world that your listener can clearly identify with.

This is the first buy-in that we mentioned in our last chapter. Can you describe a life situation that will leave them thinking: *Yes – my life is like that.*

b. The serious level

Once your listeners have gladly identified with your light-hearted example, can you use the same principle to show that sometimes **there are serious consequences if you get this principle wrong?**

c. The personal level

Your "serious level" example might already be a personal example. But this one is a key step – because this is where you will get an emotional connection with your audience. Can you describe a situation where they were personally affected by someone or something else? It's the same principle that you raised at the "light-hearted" and the "serious" level – but now you are applying it personally.

In all the messages I have ever heard that **didn't** engage me, this is the step that is most often left out. The preacher gave me no personal connection – I had no emotional commitment to where they were heading; I had no compelling reasons as to why I should engage with their destination.

Your second buy-in needs to occur somewhere here. Can you describe a real situation – where there is a real emotional response – that highlights a real problem, so that once again your audience is nodding and agreeing with you?

d. The spiritual level

Can you now describe **the same principle** and show how it affects our relationship with God? If the first three steps alerted us to the human consequences of getting this principle wrong, this fourth step shows us the eternal consequences of getting it wrong with God. This is the step that asks the spiritual question that will be answered by the rest of your message.

Often you can combine some of these steps together. The important thing is that there are at least a couple of steps to help make it easy for your listeners to commit to travelling with you on your journey.

Each of these levels offers an opportunity for your listeners to buy in, in a deeper way.

4. Intensify their desire

If your message is going to provide a solution, you first have to get your listeners to wrestle with the problem. If your Bible passage is going to provide an answer, your listeners not only need to know what the question is, **they need to want to know the answer**

for themselves. That's what I mean by "intensify their desire". Can you help your listeners to identify what their issue is so that they want to discover the biblical answer?

This is where you can secure a buy-in for the ultimate destination.

The four steps in action

In a recent Bible talk to our high-schoolers, I was preaching a message I called *"Totally Transformed Fun"*. Our aim was to investigate the Christian approach to fun, parties and alcohol. The destination I believe God wanted to take us to was this: *The greatest satisfaction we can ever have in our life is in trusting and obeying Jesus.* On the specific subject of alcohol, the Bible shows us it is a great blessing from God, but there are firm guidelines to avoid possible dangers.

My suspicion as to what our young people were already thinking about our destination was *I know God puts these guidelines in place, but surely I'm allowed to have some fun?*

In my thinking, this led me to the following observation: The number one excuse that young people give as to why they don't want to commit themselves fully to Jesus is: *I want to have some fun first.* So, asking this question: *Where is this principle (of making excuses) common in their everyday life?*, I came up with the following steps to draw them deeper into wanting to go to our biblical destination.

1. Arrest their attention

My opening line was: *Do you know what the world's biggest excuses are?*

2. Secure their agreement

My next step was to make it simple for them to agree that it is easy to make an excuse when you want to cover up the real reason for not wanting to do something.

My aim at this point was to secure their general agreement of the principle. I wanted them to "buy in" to the journey. And at every point in the next few minutes, I wanted them to buy in on ever deepening levels of commitment.

3. Deepen their engagement

a. The light-hearted level

We looked at an incident that is commonplace for today's teens. I told a story about how people often make an excuse to get out of going to something simply because they've had a better offer. You suddenly get a text message from a friend who was meant to go to the movies with you, saying: "*Sorry. Can't come. Something's come up*". A common occurrence, easy to identify with. And very annoying!

This was my next buy-in point. I wanted them to think: "*Yes! That's me!*"

b. The serious/personal level

We then took this principle to a slightly more serious – and potentially hurtful area: the excuses that guys and girls give when they want to break up with their romantic partner.

Probably every one of our teenagers has felt the pain of having someone they care about break up with them. I was hopeful that this would involve an emotional connection that would say: *Yes – I hate it when people use excuses like this, and I end up getting hurt.*

The idea was to make it easy for the youthful audience to agree: "*Yes, we make excuses all the time when we want to get out of something, and it hurts*".

Please note: If you want to get your listeners to agree that a particular action or attitude is bad or unhelpful, you need to help them feel the pain of what it is like when other people treat them in a bad way. If you want your listeners to agree that "they themselves are sinful", you first need to get them to agree that "other people are sinful".

This took their buy-in to a deeper level.

c. The spiritual level

We then looked at the excuses that young people give as to why they are not fully committed to Jesus. *"I want to have fun first"* was easy to identify as a major reason.

To intensify their challenge, I simply asked whether they had ever offered that excuse to God.

I then suggested that lying behind that question is the assumption that God's instructions in the Bible actually stop us from having fun. That is, to enjoy myself to the full, I need to break God's commands. I suggested that this attitude lay behind every sin we commit.

Once again, to intensify the challenge, I asked whether it was possible that that is what they actually believed – that they didn't trust Jesus to give them the best life possible.

This now connects their "buy-in" to my ultimate destination.

Here is my actual text at this point:

*Do you really trust that God wants the best for you? Here's what you've got to believe. That if there's something that is going to be good for you – God says: **"Do it"**. He only says: **"Don't do it"** if he knows it will be bad for you.*

*Today I want to talk with you about the one topic that is most associated with parties and fun. In most circles – it's the essential element for having fun. Most people believe **"you can't have a party without it"**. Most people believe **"you can't have fun without it"**.*

*And yet this one element causes more pain and destruction in our country than anything else. In many official reports, it's been described as **"our biggest drug problem"**. One word. Seven letters. ALCOHOL.*

Then they were ready to engage for the journey. They had bought-in to the experience big time. Then they wanted to find out what the destination was. Then they were ready for some hard-hitting words from God that would challenge their attitudes and behaviour. But if I hadn't taken the time to engage them one step at a time, they might never have signed up for the journey, and never arrived at their God-given destination.

How do I know if my Hook is effective?

At the end of your Hook, here's what you need to check: *Have I helped my listeners to discover a reason why they want to go to my destination?*

That is the purpose of the Hook: that your audience will want to engage with you. That they will want to engage with your journey. That they will want to engage with your destination. If your Hook hasn't left your listeners wanting to go to your destination, then it is unlikely that they are still travelling with you.

So in your preparation, just when you think you have nailed your Hook, ask yourself this question: *Have I helped my listeners to discover a reason why they want to go to my destination?*

Of all the messages that I get to listen to, this is the step that is most often left out.

You may be asking: *Isn't all this just modern speaking techniques? Isn't it God the Holy Spirit who changes people, and not my presentation skills? Aren't you just teaching me how to manipulate people with fine words and emotional stories?*

Good questions!

And you are right to be cautious about relying on "technique" and not on the power of the Holy Spirit wielding His sword.

But when we ask the question: *How did the biblical preachers make sure that they had their listeners on board, so they could take them to their God-given destination?,* we discover that these are the very same techniques that they used!

Next chapter!

Chapter 14

Engaging your audience – some biblical examples

have presented a suggested path to follow to help your listeners to engage with your message. But there is no set formula. There are no nifty techniques that you can learn that will guarantee that your audience is on board with where you are going.

And I'm not going to pretend that the engagement path I have suggested is a biblical mandate. There is nothing in the Scriptures that suggests you **have** to do it that way. Nor am I suggesting that every message given in the Bible follows the same formula. However, it is interesting when we look at some sermons in the Bible to see the steps that each speaker took to maximise the engagement of their listeners. Each one is different – but each time the preacher **takes the time to engage their listeners.** Each one creates their own unique Hook.

Come with me and check out three key biblical messages. Ask yourself this question: *What is the preacher doing to help engage their listeners to join them on the journey to their destination?*

1. Nathan's message to David – 2 Samuel 12

This is a tricky message to prepare. First, it's to a congregation of just one. And not just anyone. The target of this message is none other than King David, the most powerful person in the entire nation of Israel. The prophet Nathan is charged by God with the responsibility of confronting King David with his sin. David has had a sexual liaison with a married woman, Bathsheba, and has got her pregnant. To cover up his sin, David has arranged for her husband, Uriah, to be killed. These are serious charges indeed. How do you approach the ruler of the superpower of the planet and get him to agree that he should be condemned because of a major sin in his life? Imagine how Nathan must have felt! Let's listen in as Nathan raises this tricky subject.

a. Arrest their attention

Nathan does not start his message with: *I want to confront you with your sin.* He gets to that eventually. But check out how he starts:

> The LORD sent Nathan to David. When he came to him, he
> said, "There were two men in a certain town, one rich and
> the other poor."   **2 Samuel 12:1**

He starts by telling a story. A story that will no doubt arrest the attention of a king who has the affairs of the world on his mind.

b. Secure their agreement

Nathan's job is to get David to admit to the seriousness of his own sin – and to be prepared to be held accountable for the consequences. As Nathan proceeds with his story, he reaches a point where King David absolutely agrees with the principle that those who take advantage of others in a sinful way need to be held to account. Nathan describes how the wealthy farmer with huge numbers of sheep and cattle takes away the only lamb that was owned by the poor farmer. David is outraged at this injustice and cannot stop himself from bursting out:

> David burned with anger against the man and said to
> Nathan, "As surely as the LORD lives, the man who did this

deserves to die! He must pay for that lamb four times over, because he did such a thing and had no pity."

2 Samuel 12:5-6

c. Deepen their engagement and intensify their desire

Once David has agreed with the principle in general, Nathan then immediately dives deeper with David. He started with the serious level (the wealthy farmer who took the poor farmer's only ewe lamb) and now moves straight to the personal level:

Then Nathan said to David, "You are the man!"

2 Samuel 12:7

David is now confronted with his own sin. After a little more explanation from Nathan, David is now able to admit what he had been hiding all along:

Then David said to Nathan, "I have sinned against the LORD."

2 Samuel 12:13

There is much more that Nathan said in this message. But can you note the *path of engagement* that Nathan took David on:
- He arrested his attention
- He secured his agreement
- He deepened his engagement and intensified his desire

Nathan preached like a train driver.

2. Peter's message at Pentecost – Acts 2

It is now a month or so after Jesus' death and resurrection. The disciples had been hiding in fear – because the same crowd that

119

had shouted at Jesus: *"Crucify him!"* were still around and still in a hostile mood. The disciples had every right to fear for their own lives.

After the giving of the Holy Spirit, the crowd was attracted to where the disciples were gathered. They kept hearing the disciples speak – and everyone heard them in their own native language. They were intrigued. Many thought that the disciples had had too much to drink! So, in front of this hostile crowd, Peter stands up to preach to them.

What he really wants to say is: *"You killed Jesus"*. Under God's guidance, he wants them to realise the horror of their sin, and their need to face the consequences. But he doesn't start by simply saying: *"You killed Jesus"*. He will get to that eventually. But check out how he starts:

a. Arrest their attention
In one sense, God had already grabbed the crowd's attention. There had already been some spectacular cosmic effects surrounding the death of Jesus. Then, when the disciples had received the gift of the Holy Spirit, and started speaking in tongues so that everybody heard them in their own native language – you can imagine – *their attention had already been arrested!*

All Peter has to do in his opening line is to give voice to what everyone was already thinking ("they're drunk!"), and show them something far deeper than this had occurred.

> "These people are not drunk, as you suppose. It's only nine in the morning."   **Acts 2:15**

Certainly an engaging first line. I don't know about you, but I've never had to start an evangelistic sermon with the words: *We're not drunk!* But Peter had asked the right question: *What's going on in the world of my hearers?*

b. Secure their agreement

Peter now turns to the prophet Joel. His listeners would be very familiar with Joel's writings. If he can get them to agree with the *words* of Joel's prophecy, then he can take them the next step to agree with the *interpretation* of Joel's prophecy.

"No, this is what was spoken by the prophet Joel ... I will pour out my Spirit in those days, and they will prophesy ... I will show wonders in the heaven above and signs on the earth below ... And everyone who calls on the name of the Lord will be saved."　　　　　**Acts 2:16-21** *(excerpts)*

c. Deepen their engagement

Once Peter has secured his listeners' agreement with the words of the prophet Joel, he proceeds to enlist their agreement with the interpretation of Joel's prophecy. By doing this, he deepens their engagement – to a very personal and challenging level.

"Fellow Israelites, listen to this: Jesus of Nazareth was a man accredited by God to you by miracles, wonders and signs, which God did among you through him, as you yourselves know. This man was handed over to you by God's deliberate plan and foreknowledge; and you, with the help of wicked men, put him to death by nailing him to the cross.　　　　　　**Acts 2:22-23**

Peter has now confronted his listeners personally and emotionally with the words: *"You ... put him to death by nailing him to the cross"*. Ouch.

d. Deepen their engagement – again

Peter keeps going. He has just accused the listening crowd of being personally responsible for crucifying the Lord of life. But he still wants to take them deeper.

Read Acts 2:24-35. See how Peter deepens their engagement, one step at a time.

- He has used the words of Joel – a prophet familiar to them – to accuse them of the murder of Jesus.
- Then he shows how God has raised Jesus from the dead.
- This makes Jesus greater than the patriarch David (the one whom the crowd would have acknowledged as "the greatest ever").
- In fact, even David prophesied about the coming of the Christ.
- Now that God has raised Jesus to heaven, Jesus can now give the gift of the Holy Spirit to all who follow Him.

He first deepens their engagement by accusing them of the murder of Jesus of Nazareth. He then goes one more step to show them that God has raised Jesus from death. He challenges their honouring of David by declaring that even David spoke of someone greater than himself. Each step of this deepening of engagement is to produce one result – to heighten their desire to take dramatic action.

e. Intensify their desire
Peter's conclusion of his ever deepening picture of who Jesus really was climaxes with:

"Therefore let all Israel be assured of this: God has made this Jesus, whom you crucified, both Lord and Messiah."

Acts 2:36

There it is. They have killed the very person whom God had made both Lord and Messiah (Christ). This is the climax that pushes the crowd to the very response that Peter was after:

> When the people heard this, they were cut to the heart and said to Peter and the other apostles, "Brothers, what shall we do?" **Acts 2:37**

Peter gets to say what he had wanted to say all along.

> Peter replied, "Repent and be baptised, every one of you, in the name of Jesus Christ for the forgiveness of your sins. And you will receive the gift of the Holy Spirit." **Acts 2:38**

That was always the destination of Peter's message. This is the response that he wanted to see. But take note, Peter didn't **start** with his destination. He took the time to engage his listeners to **want** to take this journey with him. He arrested their attention; he deepened their engagement; he intensified their desire.

Peter preached like a train driver.

3. Paul's message at Athens – Acts 17

Paul finds himself at the Areopagus at Athens. This is where the learned scholars came to listen to the latest speakers and debate new ideas.

> All the Athenians and the foreigners who lived there spent their time doing nothing but talking about and listening to the latest ideas. **Acts 17:21**

Paul had been talking about the resurrection of Jesus. This had aroused the curiosity – and the hostility – of many of his listeners. He finally gets a chance to have his say when he is invited to speak to the assembled multitudes.

Paul had done his homework. He had already asked the question: *What's it like to live in the world of my hearers?* He had already spotted the very religious nature of the city of Athens – how there were statues everywhere dedicated to false gods.

> While Paul was waiting for them in Athens, he was greatly
> distressed to see that the city was full of idols.   **Acts 17:16**

The destination of his message was now set. He wanted to warn the Athenians about the foolishness of worshipping idols. He wanted to show them that the reason that Jesus had been raised from the dead was that he might return to judge the world. He wanted to warn the Athenians to turn from their evil, and to turn to Christ.

That was his destination. But he didn't start off by announcing it. He wanted to engage his audience first, so they were ready to hear and accept what he was saying.

a. Arrest their attention
How did he grab their attention and get them on-board? He made a simple statement that not only commended the Athenians, but showed that he understood their world.

> Paul then stood up in the meeting of the Areopagus and
> said: "People of Athens! I see that in every way you are very
> religious ..."   **Acts 17:22**

You can imagine the men of Athens poking each other in the ribs and saying: *Yes we are! Much more religious than those other cities. This guy seems to understand us.*

b. Secure their agreement
He then simply secured their agreement with his next statement:

"For as I walked around and looked carefully at your objects of worship, I even found an altar with this inscription: TO AN UNKNOWN GOD." **Acts 17:23**

His listeners would now be thinking: *That's right. We honour all the gods – but nobody can really say what God is like.*

c. Deepen their engagement
Then Paul goes for the jugular. He is going to rock the basic presupposition of his listeners.

"So you are ignorant of the very thing you worship—and this is what I am going to proclaim to you. The God who made the world and everything in it is the Lord of heaven and earth and does not live in temples built by human hands. And he is not served by human hands, as if he needed anything. Rather, he himself gives everyone life and breath and everything else. From one man he made all the nations, that they should inhabit the whole earth; and he marked out their appointed times in history and the boundaries of their lands." **Acts 17: 23-26**

Paul is going deeper with every sentence. His train of thought is: *No, God doesn't live where we tell Him to. We live where He tells us to!*

d. Intensify their desire
Paul now wants these Athenians to abandon mere statues representing their various gods, and actively to seek the one true God. This is the desire he is seeking to intensify.

"God did this so that they would seek him and perhaps reach

out for him and find him, though he is not far from any
one of us."   **Acts 17:27**

He can sense they have a desire to search after God. He intensifies
this by urging them to reach out to the true God – and that he is
not far from any of them.

e. Secure their agreement – again

Realising he is encountering opposition, he keeps working at
getting the crowd to agree with him.

"'For in him we live and move and have our being.' As some
of your own poets have said, 'We are his offspring.'"

Acts 17:28

He quotes well-known Athenian poets and writers. He knows his
listeners would agree with them. It's the ancient version of using a
line from a current rock song to emphasise your message. Having
quoted people they already trust, he draws his conclusion:

f. Intensify their desire – again

"Therefore since we are God's offspring, we should not think
that the divine being is like gold or silver or stone — an
image made by human design and skill.   **Acts 17: 28-29**

He wants to provoke his hearers to asking the question: *Well, what
is God really like?*

He is now ready to deliver his punch line:

"In the past God overlooked such ignorance, but now he
commands all people everywhere to repent. For he has set
a day when he will judge the world with justice by the man

he has appointed. He has given proof of this to everyone by
raising him from the dead."   **Acts 17:30**

That was his destination all along. But he did not start there. He
picked up his passengers from the railway station; he attracted
them to his train; he engaged them on the journey; and he took
them to his destination.

David... Peter... Paul... they weren't just men of great faith.
They each preached like a train-driver.

Chapter 15

The first principle of illustrations

L et's just check the journey so far:

- **The Hook:** is where you engage your listeners, get them on your train, and help them to commit to travelling to your destination with you.
- **The Book:** is the centrepiece of your whole message. Your biblical content dictates your destination, and is the controlling factor in your *Hook*, your *Look* and your *Took*.

And now, the next step:

- **The Look:** is where you explore your biblical content. This is where you get your listener to engage with the Scriptures. This is where you ask questions, illustrate, simplify and explain. If *The Book* is where you get the Scriptures into your listeners, *The Look* is where you get your listeners into the scriptures.

1. The purpose of illustrating

Why bother telling stories, giving examples, or illustrating ideas? Quite simply, illustrations and stories are like windows in a house. They bring light and clarity to everything in the message. Just like windows, illustrations and stories help your content to be seen clearly. They give you the whole picture. Because of your *Look*, everyone will be able to see your *Book* and your *Took* far more clearly.

Imagine a house without any windows. No matter how magnificent the contents of the house are, without any windows no-one can see it. Conversely, if a house were **all** windows, it would become unbearable. So much light would come in that it would distract you from the contents and the grandeur of the house. There might indeed be a horticultural purpose for a glasshouse – but no-one wants to live in one! In the same way – a good message will have just enough light to illuminate its contents, but not too much so that it distracts.

Great preachers will use words to paint a picture; a picture that your audience will be able to see in their mind's eye. When you can provoke your audience to use their imagination to picture something in their mind, then they will be engaged more deeply – they will see your point more vividly- and your message will become more memorable.

2. The first principle of illustrating

The essence of an effective illustration is simply this: *you take something that your audience is familiar with to explain something that they're not familiar with*. This will make an emotional connection with your hearers.

Jesus did this time and time again. He wanted to explain the kingdom of heaven (something his listeners did not clearly understand). So He used **everyday** illustrations – about farming, agriculture, cooking, trading or fishing – to explain this unfamiliar concept.

"The kingdom of heaven is like a man who sowed good seed in his field."   **Matthew 13:24**

"The kingdom of heaven is like a mustard seed, which a man took and planted in his field."   **Matthew 13:31**

"The kingdom of heaven is like yeast that a woman took and mixed into a large amount of flour until it worked all through the dough."   **Matthew 13:33**

"The kingdom of heaven is like treasure hidden in a field. When a man found it, he hid it again, and then in his joy went and sold all he had and bought that field."

Matthew 13:44

"The kingdom of heaven is like a merchant looking for fine pearls."   **Matthew 13:45**

"The kingdom of heaven is like a net that was let down into the lake and caught all kinds of fish."   **Matthew 13:47**

Remember: the essence of an effective illustration is to take something that your audience is familiar with to explain something that they're **not** familiar with.

To engage your listeners, the story that you tell **must be a common-place event for your hearers**. Something that they can picture immediately. Something that needs no explanation. If you find you have to *explain* the detail of your story – because your audience is *unfamiliar* with it – you have lost the essence of an effective illustration. You are now using a story that your audience is not familiar with to explain something that they are also not familiar with. There is no emotional connection. See the problem?

What Bible teacher in their right mind would ever do that? Sadly, there are **stacks** of them! Check out the following illustrations I have heard – which break the number one rule of an effective story – because they do not use an illustration that the audience can readily picture.

I heard a preacher about to introduce us to an important doctrine. He wanted to express how crucial it was. Here was his illustration: *"I want you to understand how important this doctrine is. It stands out like the Matterhorn"*.

This might have been a good illustration if you lived in Switzerland or Italy, and this famous mountain was sitting there in the backdrop. But this illustration was used in Sydney, Australia. Not one of us had ever seen the Matterhorn. We had barely seen a photo of it. While we *understood* what the preacher was saying, and we could imagine that it was a tall mountain, it had no real impact on us because it was a picture we were entirely unfamiliar with. Perhaps if he had said: *It stands out like Mount Kosciuszko...* (the tallest mountain in Australia), or: *It stands out like Uluru...* (that huge monolith in the centre of Australia), it would have had more impact. Probably for us Sydney-siders, the best illustration would have been: *It stands out like the Harbour Bridge...*

The Matterhorn story was an *okay* story, but it wasn't an *effective* story. We understood his illustration; we could imagine The Matterhorn; but because it was unfamiliar to us, the story had no impact. It certainly had no emotional connection.

Similarly, illustrations that start out like this are ineffective: *In the middle of Oxford there is a street with a bend in it...* or *In 1742, there was an army general...* Unless, of course, you are preaching in Oxford, where everybody is familiar with that particular street, or you are speaking to a Military Historical Society, you have now broken the number one rule of effective illustrations: you are not using something that your listeners are readily familiar with and can easily picture. You will not make an emotional connection.

You can use these sorts of *unfamiliar* stories once you have engaged your listeners on your journey. But if you want your audience members to *buy in* to where you are going, the most effective way to do this is with a story that is familiar and commonplace to them.

I was staying with a family in the southern end of Los Angeles, and one morning, as we were driving through the suburban streets, I noticed hundreds of men on the side of the road... just standing... just waiting. I enquired of my American hosts: *"What are those men doing there?"* Their answer was: *"They're illegal immigrants, and they're waiting for farmers to drive into town because they need some labourers for the day. They will put them in the back of their pickup truck and give them a day's work."* I asked: *"How long do the men stay there?"* *"Right into the afternoon. Sometimes farmers won't come in until midday. Then at least they get half a day's work."*

My Australian friend who was with me – a pastor at another church – remarked to me: *"What a great sermon illustration! This is a great story to tell to explain the parable where workers were taken to the farm at different times of the day. I can't wait to get back to my home church and use it."*

What do you think of that suggestion?

Would it have been a good illustration? I tell you where it would be a *great* illustration – with *huge* emotional impact: if you were teaching the Bible to a congregation of illegal immigrants in LA who know the pain of waiting day by day for an offer of work. Or if you were preaching to a group of Californian farmers who know the hassle of having to get extra farm-hands in the middle of the day. Then it would be a powerful example because it would use something that the hearers were instantly familiar with. It would have a powerful emotional connection. But to use it back in Australia? Perhaps it's an okay illustration, but it is not an effective one. There will be no emotional connection.

TV Shows

This is such an easy trap to fall into. Have you ever described a scene from a movie – or a TV show – to illustrate your point in a message? This could be an excellent illustration *providing your listeners have seen the show themselves!* But for your listeners who have never seen the show, your illustration is now using something unfamiliar to explain something that is also *unfamiliar*. See the problem?

This doesn't mean you *can't* describe scenes from movies or TV shows as illustrations. But I want to be convinced that at least 75% of my audience have seen the show before I use it. That can be a bit of a stretch – although it is somewhat achievable if you are preaching to an age-specific audience. If you are preaching to teenagers, and there is a new hit TV show aimed at teens that *everyone* is talking about, then you might be on safer and more effective territory.

If you want to use something on TV as an illustration, then there is something that has a good chance of having at least 75% of your audience familiar with it. *TV ads!* Simply remember the principle: you take something that your audience is familiar with to explain something that they're not familiar with. This will make an emotional connection with your hearers. This will be an effective illustration.

The worst illustration

The **least effective** illustration I've heard? This was one I was actually required to use. I was on a team that was teaching Scripture in a local public high school. I was going to take a class of Year 9 boys. We were teaching through some of Jesus' parables – and the lesson for the day was The Tenants in the Vineyard.

To explain this story about ancient Middle East farming practices (an unfamiliar concept to Year 9 schoolboys!) we were required to use the following illustration. We were given an audio recording of *The Jungle Doctor* telling a story about the *African bride-price* (The African custom of having to pay a price to a girl's father if you wanted to marry her). I'm sure it was a fascinating story, but to use an illustration from tribal Africa – to explain a story about Middle Eastern farming – it broke every rule of an effective illustration! Apart from which, it would probably result in a classroom of 30 totally disengaged teenage boys!

Just out of interest, what story would **you** use to help illustrate the Tenants in the Vineyard to 14-year-old non-Christian boys?

Okay – we've established the first principle of great illustrations: you take something that your audience **is** familiar with to explain something that they're **not** familiar with.

So – how do you make your illustrations absolutely engaging?

Next chapter!

Chapter 16

Stories that connect with your audience

I t's okay if your listeners simply understand you intellectually – but if you want them engaged on your journey, you must connect *emotionally*. That is, your listener has to identify with you. They have to want to explore your destination. They have to trust you enough to continue on your journey. They have to *feel okay* about hanging in with you. They must be *motivated* to take action.

That's why your stories and illustrations must be something that they are familiar with. Something that they readily identify with. Something that they are emotionally connected to. Something that helps them feel the pain of their problem – so they will be highly motivated to travel with you to your solution.

Check out a few stories that Jesus uses – that surely would have had an emotional connection:

"Which of you, if your son asks for bread, will give him a stone? Or if he asks for a fish, will give him a snake?"

Matthew 7: 9-10

The picture that Jesus uses – of a mum or dad feeding their kid on stones or snakes – would make an emotional connection with every parent listening. I can assure you that after that story, Jesus' listeners were engaged!

And now - an example from the Prodigal Son:

> "So he went and hired himself out to a citizen of that
> country, who sent him to his fields to feed pigs. He longed
> to fill his stomach with the pods that the pigs were eating,
> but no one gave him anything."   **Luke 15: 15-16**

Why did Jesus include pigs in his story? What difference would it have made if this boy had got a job feeding sheep? To the faithful Jewish people listening to this story, the thought that a good Jewish boy would have anything to do with a pig – an animal that was ceremonially unclean – was a repulsive thought! There would have been a strong emotional reaction at this point. Jesus engages His listeners' emotions so that they connect deeper with him as he takes them to the destination of this story.

One more:

> "But about the resurrection of the dead – have you not read
> what God said to you, 'I am the God of Abraham, the God
> of Isaac, and the God of Jacob'? He is not the God of the
> dead but of the living."   **Matthew 22:31**

Jesus is talking to the Sadducees. They did not believe in the resurrection of the dead. The destination that Jesus wants to take His listeners to is this: that there will be a day of final accounting before God – there will be a resurrection of the dead.

The story He uses to engage His listeners goes back to their books of the Law and invokes the names of their forefathers in the faith. The Jews prided themselves on being the children of Abraham – so imagine the emotional response when Jesus cast their mind back to their heroes in the faith as part of His argument. After this point, the reaction to Jesus' statement about the resurrection is not just academic or theological. Their emotions have now been engaged – which will lead to certain and decisive action.

Does this make sense? For your illustration to be effective, it must make an emotional connection with your listener. If it only makes sense intellectually, it will never engage them for the journey.

So, keep asking this question: *What is it like to live in the world of my hearers?* If you can identify what they emotionally connect with, then you can target your illustrations very strategically.

Recently at our church, I was asked to preach the same sermon to two different congregations. One meeting was mainly attended by 65- to 85-year olds; the other was mostly made up of high-schoolers and young adults. They were both doing the same series of sermons. The message from the Bible was going to be the same. But to connect emotionally, I had to think very carefully as to what would engage each particular congregation.

The sermon was from a series in Titus. I was asked to open up Titus 1:5-9 – the role of elders in a congregation. To fit in with the overall series, I needed to challenge people as to where they got their information. Who or what did they trust for reliable guidance on life? Would it come from the Bible – taught by Christ-like people who are leaders in their congregations – or would it come from less reliable sources out there in the world?

In one sense, it wasn't hard to engage the high-school and young-adult congregation. They are growing up in a world which is awash with instant information. Young people are emotionally connected with their mobile devices. Their techno-gadgets are an extension of their personalities. It wasn't hard to challenge their over-dependence on Facebook, Twitter, Google, Wikipedia and a whole host of instant information sites. We had a lot of fun exploring the dangers of trusting sources like this. By looking at our reliance on information technology, the young people were engaged from the very start.

With the older congregation, this proved to be more of a challenge. They are not overly addicted to techno-gadgets. Indeed, they are somewhat resistant to them. So, how do we engage them emotionally on what their trusted source of information is?

If you ever need to speak to elderly people, can I let you in on a secret? **They love to remember.** They love to think back to the good old days and remember the way things used to be. So that's exactly where we headed to engage them emotionally.

We looked back on how the way we get our information has changed over the decades. We looked back at Newsreel Theatres (*ask your gran if you don't know what I mean!*); being gathered around the wireless; the advent of TV; afternoon newspapers... and noted how things had changed greatly over the years. As we went down memory lane, we had an emotional connection. They were engaged – ready to take the journey with me.

Connecting emotionally is no different from what you did in your Hook. By the stories that you tell, you can get your listeners to be nodding in agreement, saying to themselves: *Yes – that describes my life. That person who is speaking from out the front understands the issues I have to face.*

We have two youth groups at our church. One for those in Years 6-8 at school (11-14 year-olds), and the other for those in Years 9-12 (15-18 year-olds). The two groups follow each other on a Friday night. On any particular night, they get the same Bible teacher and the same message. But the emotional connection of a senior-high and a junior-high student are different. We need to use slightly different stories to engage them emotionally.

With our senior highs, the big, overwhelming emotional engagement for them has to do with boy/girl relationships. This is a new world for them; it is an exciting world; it is a scary world; it is a challenging world; it is an emotionally confronting world. So a lot of our stories with our senior highs have to do with dating, romance, going-out, first kisses and moments of tenderness. This produces a rock solid emotional engagement.

So what do we do at junior high? In one sense we could tell the same stories. Illustrations about dating and romance do mean something to them. They understand what we mean. Some of them are just starting to think about this whole issue of sexuality.

But the whole boy/girl thing is not their main emotional engagement. Some are only just starting out on this scary adventure. Others won't make a beginning for many years. Our youngest kids are still in primary school. Puberty might be some time off. While they know all about the whole boy/girl thing, their primary emotional engagement lies in another relationship.

It's their relationship with their *best friend*. It's getting invited to the party. It's being in the exclusive group that gets to stay for the sleepover. It's being included in the gang at school. These are the issues that really tap into the emotional psyche of a junior high.

So at our younger youth group, the boy/girl stories from our senior-high group are usually translated into "going out with your best friend" – "being invited to the birthday party" – and "getting to stay for the sleepover". Far more emotionally engaging.

Here is the checklist we have looked at so far:

- **Your illustrations are to shed light on your content.** They get your audience to engage with the Scriptures.
- **The essence of an effective illustration:** you take something that your audience is familiar with to explain something that they're not familiar with.
- **The most effective illustrations will make an emotional connection with your hearers.**

So… what's the next step?

Chapter 17

Stories that connect with your journey

F or your stories and illustrations to be effective, they must keep connecting your audience with your journey. No use having a great story that has nothing to do with where you're heading! For your illustrations and stories to be effective, they must help your listeners to move closer to your destination.

1. Use both stories and illustrations

I have been using the terms *illustrations* and *stories* pretty interchangeably, and for simplicity, I sometimes use one term to refer to both. But they are different from each other. Each has its own strengths – and for a presentation to be effective, you need to use both.

An *illustration* is a quick comparison. A simple word picture that sheds light on your topic. They are usually quick and easy – often lasting anywhere from 5-20 seconds – and you might well have a number of these to illustrate your point. A good illustration is often a *simile* or a *metaphor* – where you compare one thing with another.

A story engages people on a journey and takes them deeper. A story is an adventure in itself – where your listeners are engaged; where they can imagine they are part of the narrative themselves. Stories have a starting point, a development – and a climax. Indeed, each story can have its own Hook, Book, Look and Took. Throughout your story, your listeners will be provoked to wonder:

What happened next? Stories don't need to be long, but generally they would take a number of minutes.

Jesus certainly used both. We have already looked at a collection of his illustrations back in Chapter 15. "The kingdom of heaven is like…" On many occasions, Jesus would take something that His hearers were very familiar with, and use it to explain something that they were unfamiliar with.

> "Therefore everyone who hears these words of mine and puts them into practice is like a wise man who built his house on the rock."   **Matthew 7:24**

> "To what can I compare this generation? They are like children sitting in the marketplaces and calling out to others."   **Matthew 11:16**

There are stacks of others. I will leave you the fun of finding them. Jesus often used an illustration – a quick comparison – to explain what He was talking about.

But He also was a great story-teller. Sometimes He didn't just use a quick comparison, but He engaged His listeners in a narrative. By taking them on a journey – he connected with them at a deeper level – and stirred their emotions in their response.

> "There was a man who had two sons…"   **Luke 15:11**

> "Listen! A farmer went out to sow his seed…"   **Mark 4:3**

> "A man planted a vineyard. He put a wall round it, dug

a pit for the winepress and built a watchtower. Then he
rented the vineyard to some farmers and moved to another
place..."   **Mark 12:1**

Jesus was a master story-teller. In the next chapter, we will look
more at what makes a story dynamic and memorable. But for now,
can you just note that for your message to be engaging – you need
both *illustrations* and *stories*.

2. Use the pictures that are already in the Bible

As you read the Bible, you will see *it is already full of great pictures!*
Both Old and New Testaments are full of vivid pictures that are
ready for the Bible teacher to take and intensify. You don't always
have to think of your own stories. Use the pictures that the Bible
already provides.

They are everywhere! Check out this picture from Isaiah:

They will be called oaks of righteousness, a planting of the
LORD for the display of his splendour.   **Isaiah 61:3**

Do you see the picture of the *oaks of righteousness*? What can you
make of that picture? Can you describe to us a mighty tree, thick
and strong, unshakeable? Why does the Bible use the term *oak* of
righteousness? What does that convey? We are not called *twigs*
of righteousness. The picture is already there in the text. Use it.
Get us to picture it; involve us; engross us; and engage us on our
journey.

Here is a picture from Jesus:

"It is easier for a camel to go through the eye of a needle
than for someone who is rich to enter the kingdom of
God."

Mark 10:25

Can you see this vivid picture? Can you see how comical it is? Your audience need to feel this. So picture for them how teeny-tiny a needle is. Now picture how miniscule the eye of a needle is. Hold up an imaginary needle to your eye and squint and strain to see it. It's pretty small!

Now imagine how gi-normous a camel is! Picture it on the platform with you. Look up at it. Walk around it. Measure it out.

Now compare the two. How hard would it be to push that camel through the eye of a needle? What about if you spread *Vaseline* down its side? (Act this out on stage). What about if you rigged it up to a four-wheel-drive vehicle, and you could drag that camel forward whether it wanted to go or not? No matter what you do, there's no way that you're going to get a big, ugly, hairy camel through the eye of a teeny-tiny needle.

You didn't have to come up with that picture yourself. It's right there in the pages of Scripture. So use the pictures that God has already provided – and move people towards their God-given destination.

3. Use stories that reveal your journey

Your illustrations and stories are not meant to be a distraction from your journey, but to be an integral part of the adventure. Your stories and illustrations are not light relief because your journey is so burdensome. When you illustrate effectively, your stories themselves will take your listeners further along the track towards your destination.

Here are some checkpoints to help you stay on track:

a. Can you illustrate each of your major points?
If you can't illustrate each of your major points, then I can assure you that your audience won't be able to either! And I don't just mean a quick ten-second illustration for each point. To be effective, I would imagine that each of your points would have a number

of quick illustrations and *at least one engaging story.* If you do not have a genuine story to help your audience picture what you are saying, then you run the risk of having a disengaged audience.

So, check your notes, and see whether you have a major story for each major point you make. And if your argument is: *"I don't have enough time for another story"*, then can I respectfully suggest that your message might have too much information in it? You will be far more effective if you say fewer things – and say them well and powerfully – rather than trying to communicate a whole stack of information ineffectively.

When I look back at my early Bible talks, I cannot believe how much information I crammed into them! It was almost as if I was trying to prove I had an extensive grasp of theology each time I preached. These days I have around half the amount of material in my sermons that I used to have. And I take far more time to make sure that my messages are engaging and that my stories are engrossing.

b. Do your stories tie in with your Hook, your Book and your Took?

The best stories are ones that tie in consistently across your entire message. Is it possible to have one over-arching story that pervades your whole journey? *(Like writing a whole book where the "train-driver" is the recurring theme!!)* Some of the most engrossing messages I have heard are where the preacher has painted a vivid image in their opening, expanded it some more in their main content, and used it as their challenge in their conclusion.

I heard a great message recently by one of the youth leaders at our church. She was speaking from 1 Corinthians 6, and making the point that your body is a temple for God. This in itself is a great picture. That when the God of this universe is selecting a temple – a house that He wants to live in He selects *our bodies.* A magnificent picture!

But she kept building on this picture. She described her situation in her own house, where she is a only a tenant who rents her place from a landlord. She made a clear distinction between the two. Her point? Sometimes we treat God as a temporary tenant in our bodies, when in fact – he is the landlord! He owns our bodies! He calls the shots!

A little later she talked about the restoration that God wanted to do in our lives. She talked about the poor self image that many of us have – that we often see ourselves as an "old dump". Continuing her story of "Make your body a spiritual house for God," she simply said: *"God doesn't see you as an old dump. He sees you as a renovator's dream."* This was another new point, but she continued with the same over-arching story.

A little later she referred to Romans 6:13 – *"Do not offer the parts of your body to sin…"* She described how she and her husband kept their home nice and tidy. But then she revealed her tidying secret. They have a *dump room*. That is, they have a spare bedroom where they dump all the things that don't fit neatly anywhere else. This is a room with a closed door – and no-one is allowed to enter. She challenged us: *"Do you have a dump room in your body – your body which is your spiritual house reserved for God? Is there a secret place where you try to hide all those sins?"* Once again, she extended her over-arching story to accommodate this new point.

This is a great example of story-telling, because her one story connects you with where you have already been on the journey, and also connects with where you are heading.

c. Do your stories tie back to the point you are making?
I once heard a preacher tell a vivid story. I was engrossed! He told a story about a particular cleaner fish – that is, a fish whose only role in life appears to be to go around and clean the garbage off every other fish it meets. He told this story dramatically. He told this story with great humour. It was a fascinating picture that he painted with his words.

When he finished his story, he moved on to the rest of his sermon. He told a great story **but he never tied his story back to the point he was making.** To this day I have no idea why he told the story about the cleaner fish. Fascinating as it was, he failed to connect it with the point that he wanted to make.

Here are four words I want you to learn. If ever you tell a story, use these four words to start your next sentence. Here we go:

"In the same way..."

These words will then connect your story back to the point you are making. Okay – you don't always have to use those four exact words, but you do need to have a connecting sentence so that your great story is used to make a great point.

Let's see how Jesus does it:

"You are the light of the world. A town built on a hill cannot be hidden. Neither do people light a lamp and put it under a bowl. Instead they put it on its stand, and it gives light to everyone in the house."   **Matthew 5:14-15**

Jesus uses some great pictures in the above quote. Can you imagine how a town on a hill – with all its lights blaring on a darkened night – would be impossible to hide? Then there's a second picture. Imagine having a lamp and putting it under a bucket! Ridiculous! Having told two great stories, the Lord Jesus then makes the connection with the point He is making:

"In the same way, let your light shine before others, that they may see your good deeds and glorify your Father in heaven."   **Matthew 5:16**

A few more examples from the master story-teller:

In Luke 15: 1-6, Jesus tells a story about a man who had ninety-nine safe sheep, and one sheep who had wandered away. (A great story!) When he finds this missing sheep, the story finishes this way:

"Then he calls his friends and neighbours together and says, 'Rejoice with me; I have found my lost sheep.'" **Luke 15:6**

The point of Jesus' story? Watch His words carefully in his next sentence:

"I tell you that in the same way there will be more rejoicing in heaven over one sinner who repents than over ninety-nine righteous persons who do not need to repent."
Luke 15:7

He then goes on to tell another everyday story:

"Or suppose a woman has ten silver coins and loses one. Doesn't she light a lamp, sweep the house and search carefully until she finds it? And when she finds it, she calls her friends and neighbours together and says, 'Rejoice with me; I have found my lost coin.'" **Luke 15:8-9**

And His point? Look carefully at how He connects it:

"In the same way, I tell you, there is rejoicing in the presence of the angels of God over one sinner who repents."
Luke 15:10

"In the same way..."

Ignore these words at your peril!

4. Use stories that reveal yourself

We have already looked in Chapter 12 at the importance of your listeners learning to trust you. That can be hard for them to do when you are distant from them on a stage or removed from them in a pulpit. But one of the ways that you can make a genuine connection with your listeners is to tell stories that reveal your inner self. Your audience will always want to know how you put things into practice. They will want to know how you struggle in your role as parent, friend, co-worker or spouse. They will be happy to learn the theory that you teach them as long as they can see that you put it into practice.

You are also the great connector between your audience and your subject. If the first principle of illustrating is to use something that is familiar to your audience, then as your listeners get to know you, **you** become familiar to them. Because your listeners are now getting to you know you, they immediately become engaged when you invite them deeper into your personal world.

Two cautions about telling stories about yourself.

a. Don't make yourself the hero of all your stories

Not every anecdote you tell about yourself should be a success story. You need to reveal your struggles. You need to reveal your weaknesses. You need to reveal your failures. Because when your listeners can see that you struggle with life just as they do, then they are engaged with you for the journey. You are no longer the theoretical but unrealistic guru who gets everything right; you are now seen as a fellow passenger and a fellow struggler with life.

So, let us know when you failed. If you want to tell a story about where someone gets it wrong – don't make your friend or your boss or your partner the fall-guy in every story. Tell us about where you have got it wrong. And tell us the lessons it taught you. And then we will want to come on this journey with you.

Apart from that, telling self-deprecating stories can be very funny! More about that later when we look in depth at humour.

b. Don't burden your listeners with information they cannot deal with

Sometimes, a speaker can leave their listeners feeling burdened or embarrassed by sharing too much of their struggles and failures, especially when apologising for things that listeners may not even be aware of. A speaker also needs to be clear about the things that they are free to share and things that it is unwise to share, especially when this involves other people. You need to check carefully what you plan to say to ensure that you are not giving away anything that should be kept private or confidential. Always get permission to tell any story that involves someone else.

Here's what we've tackled in this important chapter:

1. Use both stories and illustrations

2. Use the pictures that are already in the Bible

3. Use stories that reveal your journey
- *Can you illustrate each of your major points?*
- *Do your stories tie in with your Hook, your Book and your Took?*
- *Do your stories tie back to the point you are making?*

4. Use stories that reveal yourself

Now – how do you take all this, and make your story-telling both dynamic and memorable?

Read on!

Chapter 18

How to tell dynamic stories

The skill of the preacher is not only to proclaim the truth, but to make their message alive and engaging. As you journey on with the Look – that great opportunity to explore the Scripture, explain it, illustrate it and engage with it – how do you make your story-telling dynamic and lively?

Here are seven keys to keep both you, and your passengers, firmly on track:

1. Stick to the point

Each story you tell will make one main point. **Stick to it!** You will need to put in enough detail to make your story vivid and memorable *(see the next two points)*, but don't clutter your story with all sorts of unnecessary information.

If you are telling a story about *your first date*, and the point you want to make is: *not paying attention to someone important can have disastrous consequences*, then tell us the **part** of your *date story* that makes **that** point.

Put in the detail that will make that date come alive, and be vivid and engaging. But we might not need to know the details of what happened in your relationship three weeks before, or the precise details of the car journey, or the complications with the car-park attendant, unless these incidents are central to your main point. If the details *contribute* to your point of not paying attention to your date, then put them in. But if they are merely details that amuse or fascinate you – but don't contribute to your main point – then don't clutter up a great story with unnecessary detail.

Details *do* matter. They can make your story live! But here is the question to ask of any details you want to put in: *Do these details accentuate the point of this story, or do they distract from the point of this story?*

2. Tell your story in the present tense

When you tell a story – especially if it involves you – it can be so much more effective if you tell it as if it is happening *now*. Even though your story is in the past, tell it in the present tense.

Don't say:

I was driving my car one day, and I guess I got a bit distracted. The kids were arguing in the back seat. My wife was pointing out something she had seen out the window...

Rather, tell the same story this way:

I'm out driving my car. I'm struggling to pay attention, but you know what it's like when other people are trying their hardest to distract you. The kids are yelling and screaming in the back seat. My wife is now pointing out something unusual on the highway...

Tell your story in the present tense. Tell it as if it is happening now. The difference? *It makes it easier for your audience to engage.* As you tell it in the present tense, they are far more likely to imagine your story in their minds. They will picture what you are describing – and they will be involved and engaged.

3. Dramatise with dialogue

As you tell your story in the present tense, let your characters speak. Don't tell us about what was said. Act out and speak the part of each character. Leave the quotation marks in. Let us hear – and react to – what is actually being said by the characters in your story.

So, don't say:

My wife is telling me about something unusual she has spotted on the highway …

Rather, dramatise the story by letting us hear the dialogue:

So while I'm trying to keep my eyes on the traffic ahead, my wife yells out to me: "Look – honey – look at that car!"
"What do you mean: 'Look at that car'? There must be a hundred cars out there!"

As you dramatise your story with dialogue, your audience gets the immediacy of hearing each line as if it is happening now, and they get to have their own personal reaction to each line of dialogue. By having the opportunity to feel their own reaction, they are now far more engaged in the journey you are taking them on.

Tell Bible stories the same way. If you simply read the text, it will tell the story. But re-tell it – in the present tense and with actual dialogue – for increased impact. Many Bible stories already have dialogue in them. The story of the Good Samaritan is recorded this way:

"There was a man who had two sons. The younger one said to his father, 'Father, give me my share of the estate.' So he divided his property between them."   **Luke 15:11-12**

You have already read the text in the Bible reading. So when you're preaching from it, simply dramatise what is already there. The dialogue is already recorded for you. Simply bring it into the present tense; change your body position to represent each of the characters, and re-tell the story as if it is happening now. You can re-tell it from the point of view of one of the characters in the story. Or you can re-tell it like a narrator. Both are effective.

Here is how you might re-tell it as a narrator. Note carefully the three subtle changes: (1) it's in the present tense; (2) it's more colloquial (3) the audience is invited to react as the story unfolds.

> *"There's a guy who has two sons. The younger son is coming along now to talk with his dad. Let's listen in: "Dad, I want my share of the estate – and I want it now". Let's pause there for a moment. Imagine you are the dad. How would you feel?"*

You might like to have a go at finishing the story. How would you do it? Perhaps you'd like to tell it from the point of view of one of the characters. The dad? The older son? The younger son? Make it live – and engage your audience.

4. Stimulate the senses

If you want people to engage with your story, the more *senses* you can involve, the more likely they are to be engaged – and the more likely they are to remember the details. We all know what the five senses are:

- See
- Hear
- Smell
- Taste
- Touch

Across all the stories in your message, can you engage *all five senses* in your listeners? The more senses you engage, the more likely it is that they will become part of your story, and the more likely that your audience will journey with you to your destination.

You might not always try and involve all five senses in the one story. But let's try it in this car story. Keep in mind, that the key way to involve the sense of *touch* is with *movement*.

As I'm stuck in traffic, my wife yells at me: "Look at that outrageous car that's pulled up beside us!" It's a bright yellow, open-topped sports car with a foxtail hanging from its aerial. There are five guys in there all dressed in clown outfits. They've got heavy-metal music blasting from their sound system. And look at the enormous pizzas they're eating. My favourite! I can almost taste them from here. They smell fantastic. Freshly cooked pizzas straight from the oven. Yum! And look – now they're jumping up and down, and their car is bouncing all over the place.

Can we just check: how did we get people to picture this car by adding detail which stimulated their senses?
- **See:** *Bright yellow car; foxtail; five guys in clown suits*
- **Hear:** *Heavy-metal music blasting out*
- **Smell:** *Pizzas*
- **Taste:** *Pizzas*
- **Touch** *(movement)*: *Jumping up and down; car bouncing*

Now – you would only give detail like this if this were important to your story. And you don't have to include all five senses in every story! But I want you to see how stimulating the senses makes it easy to both picture this scene **and** to remember it.

Let's just check whether your senses were stimulated as you read this story. Without checking back for the details, can you answer these questions?
- *What colour was the car?*

- *What sort of car was it?*
- *What were the occupants wearing?*
- *How many occupants were there?*
- *What were they eating?*
- *What active movement were they doing in their car?*

You probably had no problem remembering those details. In fact, you probably remembered details that weren't really emphasised. (*Can you recall how many people there were in the car? Do you know what sort of music they were playing?*) By adding vivid imagery that stimulated your senses, you were able to remember even mundane details about the story.

You don't have to engage all five senses in every story. And you don't have to spend long on it. Sometimes ten seconds is all you need to paint a quick picture of what you are talking about. But if you want people to engage with your stories, then stimulate their senses.

5. Provoke reactions

The most important part of your message is not what you say, but what your audience hears and how they react to it. It's the thought process that is going on in their heads that will effect change in their lives.

That's why telling your stories in the present tense really matters. That's why dramatising your messages with dialogue is crucial. Because as you deliver your message – one thought at a time – your audience gets to hear what you're saying *and experience their own reactions to it.*

Imagine telling a story about a car accident, where you say: *This guy pulls straight in front of me – I have to swerve to avoid him – and then he gives me the finger, and laughs as he speeds off! If that happened to you – how would you feel?* This is the moment when you allow your listeners to have their own personal reaction to what you have just said. And it is their reaction which will have more effect on them than the words you have said.

So get your listeners to react to what you're saying. Keep putting them in the story so that they become an active participant rather than a passive spectator.

6. Emphasise with pauses

If you're going to provoke your audience to react to what you are saying, then you need to allow time to let their thought processes operate. If you ask your audience a question like: *How would you feel?*, **then give them a space to answer!** Don't just race on with your next intriguing question. Pause for a moment to let them think.

You are not having a monologue all by yourself. You are engaging your listeners in a dialogue. Even if their part of the conversation is silent, it doesn't mean that they're not taking part. By pausing, you give your listeners an opportunity to engage their thought processes – to challenge their thinking so that they might be stimulated to go to your destination with you.

Your message is not all about you. Even when you are saying nothing, your audience can still be learning something.

Pauses are brilliant every time you challenge the thinking of your listeners. Every time you make a profound point. Every time they want to laugh. Every time they want to cry. Write your pauses into your notes. And use them with profound effect.

7. Create atmosphere with your voice

The most powerful weapon for any speaker is their voice. If you've ever listened to a monotone speaker, you will realise the importance of varying your voice to keep setting the mood and engaging people's attention.

You have three basic variables when it comes to altering your voice:

- **Volume** – which can be soft or loud
- **Pitch** – which can be low or high
- **Speed** – which can be slow or fast

These are all designed to be used in conjunction with each other, but if you want to engage people, you need to ensure that your voice is backing up what you are speaking about.

If someone says to you in a very slow, soft and solemn way: *I'm really excited by this topic*, then it will not register as true with you. If it really is exciting, then that excitement should come through in their voice. And while your voice should naturally follow your emotions, for preaching you need to be more conscious of it so that the emotion you want to convey doesn't somehow get lost in the crowd.

This list is not meant to be exhaustive. Feel free to add to it. But the point to remember is this one: you can alter the mood of your message and re-engage people by *deliberately* changing your voice.

What you want to convey	Probably best conveyed by
Aggression, excitement, passion	Fast and loud – getting faster and louder as the emotion intensifies
This is serious	Low pitch and slow speed
Your most important sentence	Very soft. Whisper quiet.
Increasing tension	Keep making your pitch higher
A few key words	Loud and slow

The key word for any speaker here is *variety*. Do you naturally speak slowly and softly? Well, deliberately have some sections where you turn up the speed and volume to convey the correct mood. Or are you naturally a rapid-fire speaker? You need to intentionally have some sections where you slow down and make your pattern of speech more deliberate. *Variety* is the key.

So – a quick checklist. How can you make your messages more dynamic?

1. Stick to the point
2. Tell your story in the present tense
3. Dramatise with dialogue
4. Stimulate the senses
5. Provoke reactions
6. Emphasise with pauses
7. Create atmosphere with your voice

You are a train driver. Your job is to take your passengers to a God-given destination.

We have already explored the first three sections of this journey:

- **The Hook** – where you persuaded your passengers to get on your train
- **The Book** – where you taught them the truth from God's word
- **The Look** – where you explored, illustrated and explained the Bible's teaching

And now we arrive at the last stretch of track – the **Took**.

Fasten your seat belts... we are about to arrive at our destination!

Chapter 19

Ten steps to a great finish

The Took!

This is your destination! This is where you want to take your audience. After all your hard work – to get your passengers on your train, teach them something valuable and explore it with them – you have finally arrived!

You didn't just embark on this journey to give your passengers more information; you didn't undergo this adventure just to make your audience feel better – you started this journey to take your listeners to a destination called *gospel transformation*. As you reach this last stage of your adventure, the Took, the rest of the journey is now starting to make sense.

Do you remember what you wrote down while you were still planning this journey? Even before you penned the first word? I quote from Chapter 3:

> *"When I'm done, what do I want my audience to do differently?*
> *To think differently? To feel differently?*

Your Took is the answer to this question! You have now arrived at the very purpose for which you set out.

Your Took also answers the key question that needs to be asked of any message: *So what?* That is, if everything I have just taught is true, so what? If the information we have discovered is worthwhile, what difference is it meant to make? The failure to ask the *So what?* question is the biggest barrier to preachers actually delivering their audience to their destination. It is a question that is so easy to leave out.

In my early days as a Bible-college student, I was helping out with the youth ministry at a church. I had to do a presentation at a Bible study. The subject was: *The divinity of Christ.* I researched all the information. I lined up all my Bible verses. I worked out my theology. I have no doubt it was a fine presentation. I concluded powerfully that Jesus is indeed fully God – with all the powers of God himself. Case closed.

At the end, the minister supervising me asked a question that I had never thought of. He asked me: *"So what?"* I replied: *"What do you mean, 'So what'?"* *"Well,"* he explained, *"if Jesus is really God, what difference does it make?"*

Oops! It was a question I had never thought about. Now, when I'm preparing a message, and I think I've just about finished my notes, I write across the top of the last page: **"So what?"** This is a crucial question, because without it, you will never arrive at your destination.

Your Took is what people will take home with them. It is their personal application of everything you have said. It is what will be ringing in their ears at the end of your message. Your Took is where life change begins.

So – how can you make this the most effective it can be?

1. Make it narrow
Your whole talk has been like a giant funnel. In your Hook you started it wide – to include everyone. Your early examples were general ones.

But the whole of your message has been getting narrower and narrower. When you introduced your Book, you started to focus on what God is saying. When you explored this in your Look, you started to make it more personal. Now that you have arrived at your conclusion, you have reached the narrowest end of your funnel. You have your target lined up and you are aiming for dead centre.

2. Make it specific

The job of the preacher is to take what God has revealed and apply it to the heart of the individual. That means you need to know your people. You need to know how to zoom in close. You need to know what they're getting wrong. You need to know what needs to change.

Even if you are speaking to a group that you have never met before, you can still make your application specific. Talk early on with the organisers who invited you. Ask them the hard questions such as: *Why have you invited me to speak? What's the result that you would love to achieve? When I'm finished, what do you want your people to do differently?* If there is an opportunity to mingle with your audience before your presentation, then grab it. Observe them. Listen to them. Ask the questions that will help you identify where they need to be challenged.

Your concluding steps need to be practical. Don't make your application so vague that almost anyone could agree to it:

So – are you ready to go to the next level?

If you want to use "the next level" as your catchphrase, then your application will be tighter if you make it more specific and more practical:

*So – are you ready to go to the next level **in your marriage?***
What's the next step that you have to take to make this happen?
What is something different you can say to your husband or wife today that will bring about the change that you're after?

Look for specific areas so that you can suggest very practical, very down-to-earth steps that you are challenging your audience to take. That's why you need to get to know your listeners well. The more specific and practical you can make your application, the more powerful your message will be.

3. Make it personal

Each of your listeners might be sitting in a crowd of some hundreds, but what they're interested in is what you are saying to *them* personally. Sure, they'll think it's great that *other* people were challenged and impacted by what you have said, but they are far more concerned with what *they themselves* will learn from their time with you.

So you might have started your message by talking about *we* and *us* – so that you included yourself in everything: *This is an issue that many of us stumble with. Wouldn't it be fantastic if we could achieve a breakthrough today?* It is important to do this early on, especially if you are highlighting a problem or difficulty. Your audience needs to know that you struggle with the same things as they do.

But when you reach your conclusion, you need to make your application personal. *"What step will **you** take today?"* is much more powerful than *"What step will **we** take today?"* Don't be scared to use the word *you* in your challenge. Provided you have included yourself in the problem earlier on; provided you have shared some stories of your own failures; provided that you have revealed yourself and made yourself vulnerable – people are usually prepared to accept a final challenge that is more directive by using the word *you*.

4. Make it connect

An effective Took is one that has been anticipated the whole way through your journey. However you decide to apply your message, make sure it connects with your Hook, your Book and your Look. Your conclusion should answer the questions that you raised right back at the beginning. The way you finish will provide the solutions for the problems you identified early on. Your destination becomes the application of what was learned from your content. It is the last of all the great stories you have shared in your message.

Don't suddenly spring a surprise attack on your audience in the final minutes of your message. While your Took might indeed be hard-hitting, if you prepared your audience well, it will also be very satisfying for them.

Your Took has been your destination right from the beginning. Make sure you take your passengers every step of the way.

5. Make a memorable catchphrase[2]

Can you turn the key message of your Took into a memorable catchphrase? Rather than a rambling sentence, can you deliver a one-liner that is both punchy and striking?

Here's a great way to do it: use a *chiasmus*[3] (pronounced *ky-az-mus*). This literary device has a weird name, but you will instantly recognise it when you see it. Here are a few examples; see if you can work out the essence of a *chiasmus*:

"When the going gets tough, the tough get going."
"Comfort the afflicted, and afflict the comfortable."
"Are you motivated by the love of power, or the power of love?
"Stop telling God how big your storm is.

          Start telling your storm how big God is!"

---

2 See also Chapter 25

3 This is not the same as a classical *chiasmus*, which is a far more complex literary form. Indeed there is an argument that the construction I am suggesting is technically an *antimetabole*. But in modern language construction, *chiasmus* appears to be the accepted term. American journalists like to call it a "Reversible Raincoat".

"Those who exalt themselves will be humbled, and those who humble themselves will be exalted."

Matthew 23: 11-12

"But many who are first will be last, and many who are last will be first."
Matthew 19:30

Got it? A *chiasmus* is where you repeat a phrase with the word order reversed. It comes from the Greek letter "*chi*" which is the equivalent of our "*X*". *Chiasmus* literally means: *shaped like a cross* ... or ... *marked with an X*. It's where two words or phrases cross over to make a very powerful and memorable impact.

Here's the formula for the crossover:

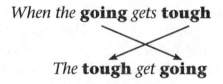

Your two key words – or phrases – *cross over* to produce a point that is hard-hitting, punchy and memorable.

You don't have to come up with a quote of the day in every message, but take the time to look at your main application. Can you re-word it to make it more punchy, more memorable and more hard-hitting?

6. Use the power of repetition

If you can get your application message down to a short phrase or sentence, then repeat it at the end of each of your sections. If you have three examples, can you use your catchphrase at the end of each of them? By using it at least three times, you will help your audience to be challenged by it, and to remember it.

7. Use the power of crescendo

If you have a strong point to make, can you make it three times in a row, with each one being more powerful than the one before it? Each sentence will be almost the same as the one before it – with a word or two changed to bring out the increasing emphasis.

Here's an example:

- *What difference will you make to your life today?*
- *What difference will you make to your friends today?*
- *What difference will you make to your world today?*

Note that, in a *crescendo*, you repeat *every word in the sentence*. This is where spoken English is different from written English. If we were writing the above three lines, we would have done it this way:

What difference will you make today to your life, your friends and your world?

But don't say it like that! The power of a crescendo is in the rhythm generated by repeating the whole sentence.

8. Don't keep it all to the end

While it makes sense to *finish* your message with your Took, there is no need to save *all your application* to the end. It can be very powerful to apply your message *as you go through it.* Have you just taught an important point in your Book section? Then apply it there. Have you just raised an interesting question in your Look section? Then apply it to people's lives while it is fresh in their minds.

If you have carefully applied God's word to people's hearts as you have been preaching, then your final Took can focus on the one big challenge that you want to be ringing in everybody's ears.

9. Nail your closing line

What are the two most important lines in any message? Your opening line; and your closing line. These are the ones you must get right. These are the ones you have scripted carefully. These are the ones that you will not change no matter what else happens in your message. Your opening line is your *take-off*; your closing line is your *landing*. Your opening line commits your audience to the *journey*; your closing line commits your audience to the *destination*. Your opening line arrests their *attention*; your closing line drives home the *transformation* you have been working towards. Without these two, your message is a journey to nowhere.

So think carefully about your closing line. What will you say? How will you say it?

Here are my three favourite ways to close a message. I've included examples of each. Not because they're necessarily brilliant, but because they might inspire you to do even better!

a. A challenging question

I often like to issue a final question which is a personal challenge to each listener.

Here's my closing line from a recent men's conference I spoke at:

> *"Will you step up to the plate and be the man that God has called you to be?"*

This is my closing line from a recent message at our youth camp:

> *"Tonight - will you say to Jesus: 'Yes – no matter what'?"*

b. A repeat of your catchphrase

If you have developed a catchphrase – either throughout your whole message, or just for your conclusion – it can be very effective to simply repeat this catchphrase as your final line.

This is how I concluded another message that had a central catchphrase throughout:

"We're not spectators – we're players!"

At a recent sermon on "Giving", I repeated a catchphrase, and then turned it into a challenging question:

God gave up everything He had
    – to give you everything you've got.
God gave up everything for you.
    Will you give up everything for Him?

c. Repeat your main points as challenging questions.

If you've had clear and concise main points throughout your message, then a good way to finish is to repeat your main points as challenging questions.

At a recent presentation to professional speakers, I had made four key points throughout my message. I finished my presentation by repeating each point as an action-based challenge:

At your next presentation
    – will you get your audience on your train?
At your next presentation
    – will you take them to your destination?
At your next presentation
    – will you take them to a place where they've never been before?
At your next presentation – will you speak like a train driver?

10. Don't just stop – FINISH!

You know how frustrating it is when your train just suddenly stops? You're not at your destination; you're not even at a station. You're just stuck in the middle of nowhere.

Don't let your messages end this way. Don't just stop – **finish!** Make sure that you bring your message to a conclusion. Make sure that you take your passengers all the way to their destination. And make sure that for every passenger, you have made the journey worthwhile. That's what good train drivers do!

Chapter 20

Finishing with God's power

P reaching from God's word is never a merely human exercise. Finishing a sermon is not just a man-made activity. Applying God's word is not based on human strength. We are dealing with God, who is omnipotent. We are conveying God's word which is living and active. We are proclaiming the gospel of Jesus, which is the dynamite of God to save those who believe. We are displaying the power of God's Spirit, who will convict the world of guilt in regard to sin and righteousness and judgment.

Having a powerful application – a memorable Took – does not ultimately depend on the brilliance of your public speaking, but on the power of God, who can change anyone's life.

Listen to what Paul says:

> My message and my preaching were not with wise and
> persuasive words, but with a demonstration of the Spirit's
> power, so that your faith might not rest on human wisdom,
> but on God's power.　　　　　　　**1 Corinthians 2: 4-5**

So, how do you conclude your message in a persuasive way that points to God's power?

1. Choose your weapon carefully

"Comfort the afflicted, and afflict the comfortable."[4] While that saying was originally coined to describe the power of newspapers, it contains wisdom that is well kept in mind by Bible teachers. The word you speak is a double-edged sword. Your words have the power both to comfort the afflicted and afflict the comfortable. You need to know your listeners well enough so that you apply your message the right way.

If you've been speaking on Proverbs 6 – the hard-working ant and the danger of laziness – you need to know the people you are speaking to. Can you see that your application will be very different depending on whether you are speaking to:

- a group of people who are lazy, *or* ...
- a group of people who are over-busying themselves at work or Christian ministry.

Most likely you will have both groups in your audience; those who need afflicting and those who need comforting. You need to express your application wisely, so that those who need comforting are not afflicted and burdened with guilt, and those who need to be shaken out of their comfort zone hear the words that are meant for them.

2. Keep it prophetic

In a biblical sense, the application of your message is meant to be *prophetic*. Now as soon as I mention the word *prophetic*, I know I will trigger strong and varied reactions in a whole variety of readers. Some of you will be thinking: *We don't do prophecy at our church*; others will think *Wasn't that just in the Old Testament?"*; while many more will be very comfortable because: *We do it all the time.* I have seen godly authors who describe prophecy as something which is wild and wacky, while others almost seem to equate it with straight Bible-teaching.

---

4   This quote is usually attributed to Finley Peter Dunne (1867-1936), journalist.

So, can I try and keep this word *prophetic* at a reasonably simple level? In the Bible, a prophet takes the word of God that has already been revealed, and applies it to the lives of individuals. We're not talking about the *authoritative* ministry of Old Testament prophets, but the *supportive* ministry of New Testament prophets:

But the one who prophesies speaks to people for their strengthening, encouraging and comfort.

1 Corinthians 14:3

That's the New Testament prophetic edge. When used correctly, people are strengthened, encouraged and comforted.

A prophet takes the word of God that has already been revealed, and applies it to the lives of individuals. As preachers, you are doing a similar thing. Your job is not just to explain what the Bible means; your job is to help each individual to apply it to their own life. When preaching loses this prophetic edge, nobody arrives at their destination.

3. Keep it sharp

The world has far too many Bible teachers who simply want people to like them. They will say nice things. They will make their audience feel good. They will be careful not to offend them.

But God's word was never designed to be nice and inoffensive.

For the word of God is alive and active. Sharper than any double-edged sword, it penetrates even to dividing soul and spirit, joints and marrow; it judges the thoughts and attitudes of the heart. Nothing in all creation is hidden from God's sight. Everything is uncovered and laid bare before the eyes of him to whom we must give account.

Hebrews 4: 12-13

God's word is sharp and penetrating. Incisive. Painful at times. Your *Took* might need to be the same. As long as you have included yourself in the list of those who fail, it is okay to be strongly challenging as you call people to change their lives to match up with the standards of God's holy word.

But might that hurt some people? Possibly. But maybe it needs to. You know when you go to the doctor for a check-up – they prod and poke and observe and measure. And as they prod and poke their way around your body, it is possible that they will touch a tender point, and hurt you. *Ouch!* you yell out in pain. *Quit prodding – that hurts!*

There are two explanations as to why you might be hurting. Perhaps the doctor has pushed too hard. Maybe they weren't careful enough. They might have been a little rough and not sensitive enough to your feelings. I'm sure this happens sometimes. But there is another possible explanation: the pain that you are feeling as a result of the doctor's prodding and poking, is because *they have discovered a problem that needs dealing with.*

Teaching the Bible can be like that. Sometimes people will hurt because the preacher pushed too hard. Maybe they weren't careful enough. They might have been a little rough and not sensitive enough to people's feelings. I'm sure this happens sometimes. But there is another possible explanation: sometimes people will feel discomfort when the preacher is applying God's word because *they have discovered a problem that needs dealing with.*

We looked at these messages earlier in this book. Listen to the concluding sentence in Peter's first sermon on the day of Pentecost:

> Therefore let all Israel be assured of this: God has made this Jesus, whom you crucified, both Lord and Christ." **Acts 2:36**

Note carefully his words: *"God has made this Jesus, **whom you*** *crucified...*". Peter didn't pull any punches. He knew that some of the people who were standing there before him had been in the crowd some six weeks earlier, shouting out: *"Crucify Him! Crucify Him!"* He doesn't make excuses for them. He doesn't water it down. He calls it as it is.

Listen to the prophet Nathan as he starts to conclude his message to King David:

Then Nathan said to David, "You are the man!"

2 Samuel 12:7

He knew what God's word said. He knew what David had done. While your sermons will probably never be this personal, don't hold back from making your application – your *Took* – specific and pointed.

Don't be scared. Make it sharp.

4. Keep it grace-filled

If people feel convicted simply because of your brilliant oratory, then you will only ever achieve a human result. If your audience are moved to respond merely because you keep applying more and more pressure, then these are not genuine responses. We do the preaching: God achieves the result. The power is not in us; the power is in God's Spirit. God does not achieve our repentance by loading us with guilt; He achieves our repentance by showering us with grace.

If you're aware that you are pressing on a tender spot, then you need to emphasise strongly God's grace and forgiveness. I have the honour of regularly teaching God's word to teenagers. If I am speaking about sexuality, I need to be aware that for many teens this is a particularly sensitive area. Many will struggle; many will fall; many will feel a deep sense of guilt. I don't think I have ever talked about sexuality with high-schoolers without emphasising God's grace and forgiveness. To ignore this would be to do a disservice to your listeners. To disregard this runs the risk of taking your passengers to the *wrong* destination.

So even though I want to keep my application sharp, personal and punchy, I still need to deliver those messages in an atmosphere of grace. The invitation to repentance is delivered inside the envelope of forgiveness. The call to change your life is contained within the framework of faith. The ultimate challenge for any Bible teacher is to trust God's word to achieve God's results in God's strength. The alternative is that I will be satisfied in declaring my own word to achieve my results in my strength.

Only one of these will really change lives. Only one of these will influence people's eternities. Only one of these will genuinely take your passengers to their God-given destination.

Chapter 21

How to use the whole stage

Now we've taken you on the entire journey, can we check through some key concepts that will take your preaching to the next level? The issues in this section are the skills you need to develop in the art of being an excellent speaker. These are techniques which, when properly employed, will help you to be effective in your communication so that you reveal the passion and the truth of God's written word.

You might be thinking: *why do I need any "techniques"? Can't I just let God's word speak for itself?*

I believe there is a call on every Christian to be the best they can possibly be in God's service. The Scripture says:

> Whatever you do, work at it with all your heart, as working
> for the Lord, not for human masters.   **Colossians 3:23**

When you work at something with all your heart, you do it to the very best that you can. If you are working for the Lord, you want to do it with a high level of excellence. If you were a worship singer, as well as deepening your heart of worship, you would also want to train your voice and learn to sing well. If your ministry is to feed the hungry mob at church events, then as well as being Christ-like, you would want to sharpen your cooking skills so your food is the most delicious it could possibly be.

The same is true for a Bible teacher. You need to humble your heart and be Christ-like in your devotion; and you need to be faithful in the way you understand and teach God's word. But you should also want to learn the skills to proclaim God's word in a way that is most *effective*. This section will help you do just that.

Ministries that impact people powerfully are those that are both *faithful **and** effective*. These two qualities do not work against each other. They go hand in hand to produce a lasting effect.

So, let's walk together as we develop the art of being effective communicators. Here's the first issue we will look at: **how to use the whole stage.**

You've no doubt worked out by now, that standing rigidly behind your notes is not necessarily the way to deliver your message with maximum impact. If your message is engaging and dynamic, then that will never be reinforced by a static and frozen speaker. I'm sure you've got the message by now – if you want to move people with your message, then you've got to move!

But there is an opposite and equally dangerous habit that has now developed among some preachers – **aimless wandering!** I have seen some speakers set out on a four-kilometre walk during their message. They walk to the right; they shuffle to the left; they amble to centre stage; endlessly moving about and never stopping anywhere.

If you're going to move while you are speaking on the platform, then **move with purpose**. That is, there has to be a reason for why you move from one place to the next. Here are some guidelines to help you use your stage area in a way that will maximise your message:

1. Create mood with your body

I guess the favoured position for preachers is standing up. Is there any other choice?

Well, yes there is. *How* you stand can create a different mood.

If you decide to do something *different* from standing, that can also increase the impact on your audience's perception. So think about your stature and your gestures – and learn how they can contribute to making your message dynamic.

Different ways of standing can communicate different things. Vary *how* you stand to increase the impact of your content. Different gestures and ways of standing can mean different things at different times. The important thing to note is how *changing* your stature or gesture can help alter the mood of your message.

The following list is not meant to be exhaustive; you could probably add many more things. But have a look at these suggestions – see if you can add your own thoughts:

Feet and hands	What it might communicate
Standing behind the lectern	Tradition and authority
Moving away from the lectern	More conversational; more approachable
Standing with palms facing upwards	More vulnerable, open
Standing with arms out wide	All embracing; signifying the immensity of something; perhaps a note of celebration
Standing – one arm in the air	Triumph; *"Yes!"*
Standing – pointing at audience	A point of challenge or application
Standing – exaggerated shrug of shoulders, arms bent, facing upwards	Indecision. Frustration. Uncertainty. *"What's up?"*
Leaning against something	Very relaxed, very comfortable
Sitting on a stool	It's time for a story; or perhaps to voice an opinion.
Sit on the edge of the stage	This is very personal; Very serious
Sitting on a sofa	Very relaxed; very chatty

The key here is that you can *make* a gesture mean something by consistently using that gesture in a particular way. For example, if you are reading from a story in a book, and every time you return to this you sit on a stool, then you are communicating to your audience that sitting on a stool means you're about to look at more of the story. From that point onwards, each time you sit on the stool, your audience is already primed for what is about to happen next.

Please note that gestures change according to the size of your audience. In simple terms, the bigger your audience, then the more *exaggerated* your gestures should be, and the longer you should hold each one.

If you have an audience of ten, then you can communicate joy by simply beaming a big smile on your face. But if you have an audience of thousands – who have no hope of perceiving your every facial gesture – then you would communicate joy by exaggerating your smile – and throwing your arms around in excitement – and dancing enthusiastically – and... You do whatever it takes to communicate – and the more listeners you have, the more exaggerated your gestures need to be.

Similarly, gestures for large crowds need to be held for much longer, or they will be missed. If you are just talking with a few people, and you shrug your shoulders and bend your arms upwards in the classic *What's up?* gesture, then it will probably last for around one second. Anything longer would look inane. But if you're speaking to a crowd of thousands – a one-second gesture would be completely missed by them. With a large crowd, you might throw you hands up in the classic *"What's up?"* gesture – *and leave that gesture frozen for ten seconds*. You can even keep speaking while you hold this frozen gesture. You simply need to give people time to experience the mood you are creating by your stature and gestures.

2. Move and then STOP

Don't be an endless wanderer. To maximise your impact, walk from one part of the platform to another position **and then stop for a few minutes**. Speak from this new position for a while – and then move to another point – **and then stop again.** Otherwise your audience will grow restless as you endlessly pace like a nervous expectant father.

3. Don't look at your feet

One of the pitfalls of walking from one part of the platform to another is that there is a tendency for speakers to look at their feet as they walk. There is some logical explanation for this. You want to make sure that you don't trip over a fold-back speaker, disappear down some steps or fall off the edge of the stage! But don't do it! Of course, make sure that you can see any hazards as you commence your walk, but the whole idea of moving to a different part of the stage is to engage the audience better. You will not achieve this if your eyes are glued to the floor! Make sure that your walking on stage increases your interaction with the audience, and doesn't decrease it.

There is also a psychological tendency that lies behind this "looking at my feet" syndrome. There is a widespread belief that your short-term memory is stored somewhere near your feet! When people want to remember something that they've forgotten, they instinctively look at the floor – believing somehow that the notes they need to jog their memory are in fact taped onto their shoes. You know this is not true. It is simply a habit that many of us fall into.

To overcome this trap, simply re-arrange where your short-term memory is stored – and get into the habit of *looking at the back of the audience* to jog your memory on what comes next. If you change your habit, you will not fall into the trap of the eternal floor-gazers.

4. Know your left from your right

It is very confusing for an audience when the speaker says: *And over here on my left...* and then they walk to the right! Well, from the *audience's* point of view, they *did* walk to the right. The speaker (facing toward the audience) did indeed move to their *left*. **But they are the only person in the room to have that perspective.** For everybody else, left and right are reversed.

Doing things in line with the audience's point of view will not come naturally to you. Practise it. Say: *I want everyone to hold up their right hand*– and as you say it, hold up your left hand. Practice saying: *And over here on the left* – and then walk to the right. The more you practise, the more you'll get the hang of it.

And why does this matter?

As far as the audience is concerned, everything starts on their left, and finishes on their right. That's the way our writing goes. That's how every chart and graphic works. That's the way most people expect everything to go. **Just keep remembering that for you, the speaker, everything is reversed.** Every journey starts on your right (the audience's left) and finishes on your left (the audience's right).

To simplify things, I will now describe everything from the speaker's point of view:

a. Describing a journey

If you are on stage, and you're describing how to start a journey, you start the journey on your right and finish it on your left. If you did it the other way round, it doesn't make sense to the audience.

b. Emphasising words

If you want to emphasise a key phrase by punching out each word, and pointing to each word in logical order, your first word must be on your right. If your key phrase is: *Never give up!* and you want to point to each word so they make a logical sentence, when you say the word *Never*, you will point to your right; when you say *give* you will point to the centre; and when you say *up* you will point to your left.

c. The past and the future

Things in the past are always on your right. Walk there and tell the story. Things in the future are always on your left. Walk there and tell that part of the story.

d. The good and bad

Things that are bad are always on your right. Things that are good are always on your left. If you reverse this, it just won't make sense to your audience.

The principle is simple: for the audience, everything starts on their left and moves towards their right; for the preacher, this simply means that everything is reversed. Keep starting your journey on your right and take the audience to your destination on your left.

5. Engage each section of your audience

If you are working in a very small space, and speaking to a very small audience, this won't matter that much. Simply look at each person's face at some stage. As the whole setting is so small, each member of the audience probably already feels some intimacy with you.

But when you start speaking to hundreds, or thousands, then you run the risk of audience members feeling no intimacy with you whatsoever. By moving to different parts of the stage, you present yourself more intimately to people sitting in the corresponding sections of the audience than if you had stayed in the centre the whole time.

Of course, if you move right to one side of the stage, don't forget the people who are now way on the other side. Simply use your outstretched arm (the one closest to the people who are now furthest away) to draw them in. Use your outstretched arm to point to the people who are furthest away, and by this simple action, you will include everyone.

In addition, keep engaging everybody by regularly looking at different sections of your audience. Can you get on stage before anyone arrives and just see what it looks like from the speaker's point of view?

I regularly speak at my church, and there are four major blocks of seating for the congregation – spread in a very wide fan shape. I look at each block; I look at the front half of each block, and the back half of each block. That gives me eight different areas. It's not that hard. Just make sure you are looking at a different group of faces each time you engage your audience throughout your message.

There are areas that speakers tend to ignore. If the venue you are speaking in has a balcony or two, you need to include them. Many churches and buildings have a space for people to sit *behind the speaker*. It may contain the choir, the band or other members of the congregation. But they need to hear God's message too! Turn to look at them at least once during your talk.

But let me alert you to two more areas that speakers often ignore:

a. The front row
Can you believe that the people in the front row are often overlooked? Especially if your stage is elevated. So, don't leave them out. Look straight down every now and again and engage the front row.

b. The video camera
If your message is being videoed – and especially if audience

members are going to be watching you live on a screen – *then you must include the video camera as a crucial section of your audience.* For part of the time, look directly at it! If a large section of your audience will mainly be watching you on a giant screen – and you don't look at the camera on a regular basis – then you will never look directly at all the screen-watchers.

Even if there is no live screen for people to watch, but your message is being recorded for future on-screen or DVD use, then still include the camera as a key section of your audience and look directly at it for at least some of the time. Then you will better engage your audience who will watch you at a later date.

6. Create lasting "holograms"

One of the keys to moving with purpose is that you can create a lasting hologram by locating a particular story on its own special spot on the stage. When you tell a particular story in its own special spot, then in the audience's mind, they can still "see" that story for the rest of your message. You can look back to that spot and the story you told there will still be "visible" in people's minds. That's what I mean by creating a lasting hologram.

For example, let's imagine that you're telling a story about a teenage boy. There are two key relationships that are influencing him. One: a rather difficult relationship with his argumentative dad. Two: a very understanding relationship with his girlfriend. He finds great solace in this, but his father does not approve.

How can you create holograms so you can keep referring to these relationships throughout your message?

The difficult relationship with his dad. Where would you place that on the stage? Probably stage **right** (that is, *your* right), as it is a difficult relationship. Walk to a particular spot on stage right. Tell the story. Let the characters speak. Keep the quotation marks and use the dialogue. Act out the part of each of the protagonists.

Now move to a completely different part of the stage for the relationship with his girlfriend. Probably stage **left**, as it is a helpful and positive relationship. Tell that story there. Act it out – and create a hologram in its own stage space that you can refer to later.

Having created those two holograms in two different spaces on the stage, you can now refer back to them **without having to retell the stories**. If you want to refer to the difficult relationship with the boy's dad – simply point to the hologram you created on stage right and say something like: *What do you imagine dad would think of that?"* And by simply pointing to your previous hologram, your listeners immediately reconnect with your earlier story about their fractious relationship. Similarly, you can refer to the relationship with his girlfriend by pointing back to that hologram on the left at any stage.

You can set up an interplay between your two holograms. If you are further developing the relationship with the girlfriend, and the boy asks: *But how will I tell dad?*, all you need to do is look back over to the other side of the stage and all the emotions regarding his dad are brought to the forefront of your listeners' minds.

What if you wanted to resolve these two relationships? What if you wanted all three people to get together? Then you can go to one hologram and walk the "person" across to the other side.

This simple principle of *creating holograms* with your stories will add real impact to your messages, and give real purpose to your movement on stage.

You can use simple holograms for normal dialogue between two characters. Rather than just telling us what they are saying, stand in a slightly different place for each character. It can be as simple as looking in a slightly different direction. You can use this method for illustrating a Bible story. Simply change your position for each person so that your audience can easily picture all this in their minds.

If you want a sermon that is dynamic, you can't have a preacher who is static. Use the whole stage – and engage the whole audience.

Chapter 22

How to engage people with humour

Not every message has to be funny. God has not called us to tell jokes. He has called us to tell the world about Himself. But over the decades I have been preaching, I have discovered the very vital role that humour can play in a message. If you want to be an effective speaker, you need to understand how to make humour work for you – to help you to take your passengers to their destination.

Not everyone has to be naturally funny. Some people find it easy; folk start laughing as soon as their first words have left their mouth. But for most of us, we need to learn steps so that our humour can be genuinely effective. Whatever you think of your own attempts at humour (and perhaps, more importantly, whatever anyone else thinks of your attempts at humour!), this principle is true: *anyone can learn to be funnier than they are now.* Anyone can learn how to use humour better.

1. Why humour works

The value of humour? Quite simply – it's the easiest way to engage someone's emotions.

a. It warms people to you

It's easy to like the person who is making you laugh. It's easy to relax when you're having a quiet chuckle. The person who is laughing with you is more likely to want to go where you're going. If you want people to consider travelling with you on your train, then humour is a great way to engage them.

b. It disarms people's defences
Have you ever tried to speak to someone who simply did not want to listen? They sit there in the audience with their arms folded and a scowl on their face, using every bit of non-verbal communication to let you know: *I'm not going to listen to a word you say!* If people will laugh with you, they are more likely to listen to you. Laughter has a sneaky way of getting under our defences and opening us up to new journeys and new possibilities.

c. It connects emotionally
Back in Chapter 12 we looked at the importance of making an emotional connection with your audience in the first few minutes; the sort of connection where your listeners will be thinking: *That speaker up the front understands my life. I like them. I am happy to travel with them for a bit.* If you do not make this emotional connection early in your message, it will be much harder to persuade people to journey with you.

The easiest and most productive way to engage people emotionally is with humour. Once you have tapped into their funny bone, you have access to many other parts of their emotions.

d. It connects easily with other emotions
Often in our fast-paced world, we keep our emotions deeply hidden. We don't want to reveal too much of ourselves to others because we don't want to be vulnerable. We don't want to be hurt. For many folk these days, it's a bit of a struggle to connect with their own emotions because they are buried so deeply. But once people have opened up their emotions with laughter, they have ready access to a wide range of other deeper feelings as well.

Nothing portrayed this better than the old TV show M*A*S*H. Set in the Korean War, the series showed the horror and the futility of battle. It is set in a mobile hospital close to the front-lines of battle, where the staff deal with an endless stream of wounded soldiers, inadequate medical facilities, horrific injuries and ongoing, needless deaths. The series was written as a protest against the Vietnam War, which was raging at the time M*A*S*H was made and first screened.

And yet M*A*S*H was a comedy! The vehicle for stirring up emotions about a senseless war is laughter. If you ever get the chance to watch an episode, note carefully what happens. An outrageously funny scene is quickly followed by a scene of blood-filled devastation. I find myself going from loud laughter to quiet tears inside thirty seconds. My emotions are exposed by the laughter, so I am ready to feel the deeper emotions of pain.

Wise use of humour in your Bible teaching can help your listeners to tap into deeper emotions which will connect them powerfully with the journey and the destination.

2. The essence of humour

When I was talking with Ken Davis[5] – a brilliant comedian and communicator – he gave me the best analysis of humour I have ever heard:

> *"There are three elements in humour. Humour is real life – plus exaggeration – plus surprise."*

That is, tell a story which is a real story about something that actually happened to you. Whatever the funny bits are in that, overstate them and exaggerate them to emphasise them. And then add a twist at the end – the surprise ending that no-one was expecting.

---

5 Check out Ken Davis' excellent book – *Secrets of Dynamic Communication* – TEC Publications, 1991

This is called *observational humour* and it can be your best friend as a speaker. It is the *opposite* of telling a joke. It is not an artificial set-up. It is real life – and everyone recognises that. But by looking at things a little differently, you get to show the humour in an everyday situation.

This is the essential difference between a *comic* and a *comedian*. A comic says *funny things*; a comedian *says things funny*. That is, a comic tells jokes. A comedian brings out the humour in everyday situations. Your aim is to be more of a comedian and less of a comic.

This saves you from the nightmare problem for anyone attempting humour: *What if nobody laughs?* If you set up a joke, and the punch line falls flat, everyone knows that your humour has failed. If you start a story with: *Let me tell you a joke* or *I heard a really funny story* or *You'll roar with laughter at this one,* then you are setting yourself up to fail. You've just announced to everyone that this will be really funny – so if it isn't, everyone knows the whole thing has fallen flat.

But if you simply start telling a story, no-one knows whether it will be funny or not. When you get to the bit where you thought there would be a laugh – and nobody laughs – that's okay! As far as the audience is concerned, it is still a good story. It doesn't matter if they don't laugh. You simply move on to your next point.

The thing that actually brings the laugh is the surprise. In the next chapter, when I present my favourite humour techniques, notice how many of them depend on the surprise.

3. How to polish your humour

Here are some simple steps to help improve your use of humour – so that you will better engage your listeners for the journey.

a. Draw on your own life experiences

If you're just starting out at public speaking, and you have very little experience, you might have to include some other people's stories. Stories that you heard someone else use. Stories you read out of a book. Stories you grabbed from the internet. If you must use these, don't pretend they happened to you. You need to maintain integrity with your listeners. You can always start with: *"I heard a story about a man who..."*

Your best stories will always come from your own life experiences. Something that happened to you at the shops. Something you overheard somebody say. Something you saw on TV.

The two best places to go for these stories? Your childhood and your family life. If you want to tell a story about almost anything, you will probably find an example somewhere in these two areas. Certainly, if you want to tell a story about something stupid you did, your own childhood should be a gold mine of examples.

Warning: If you're talking about people who are known to your audience (eg: your family), be very careful not to paint them in a bad light. Tell stories from your family life where you get it wrong – not where your partner or children get things wrong. If I am telling a story about anyone else in my family, I want to make sure of two things. One: that it honours them. Two: that I have their permission.

b. Use self-deprecating humour

Your audiences will love it when you make fun of yourself. They will love to know about the stupid things you did, the bad mistakes you made, and the dumb ideas you had. Go on – laugh at yourself; everyone else will anyway, so you may as well join them.

c. Don't laugh at your own humour

If you just keep giggling while you tell your story... or if you have a cheesy grin all over your face as you get to the punch-line – then you spoil the element of surprise. You are simply telegraphing to your audience that something really funny is about to happen

– and you take away from the shock value of your punch line. Stories are much funnier when you can deliver them with a deadpan face.

d. Build the anticipation
Tease your audience. If you have misdirected their thinking intentionally, then keep them in suspense for as long as possible. If you are leading them down a garden path, then save the surprise for the end. Learn to pause at the right moment. Give them space to make their own connection in their head.

e. Keep your punch line till last
Remember how *surprise* is one of the key elements of humour? Keep your audience in suspense as long as possible. If you can, do not deliver the killer word or phrase until the very end of the last sentence. Save the surprise until last.

f. Don't explain your punch-line
If people don't *get* your joke, then just move on. Don't try and explain it. If you have to explain your punch line, it will never be funny. Just chalk it up to experience and change your story for next time. Similarly, don't repeat or add anything to your punch-line. Say it; deliver it; allow the audience to react – move on.

g. Avoid the "groaners"
Sometimes these are called "dad jokes". They're the jokes that are far more likely to elicit a "groan" than a genuine laugh. As Ken Davis once pointed out to me: *"When people are groaning, it means they're in pain"*. Puns almost always fall into this category.

There is a definite psychology behind groaners. You know those jokes that you find on bubble-gum wrappers or that come out of crackers at Christmas? They are always a very weak joke – a "groaner".

Q: Why was Santa's little helper feeling depressed?
A: He had low elf-esteem.

The psychology behind this is: they are intentionally weak to unite the whole household in groaning about how bad they are. These jokes are actually so bad they draw people together. But you do not want the whole of your congregation united because they are groaning against you!

h. Engage the audience's imagination

What's the difference between a TV drama and a radio drama? In the TV drama, everything is visualised for the audience. In a radio drama, the listener has to use their own imagination to picture what is being spoken about.

One of the brilliant things about humour is that you can use words to help your listeners to visualise an extremely funny situation. By imagining it themselves, they will appreciate the humour far more. You will really engage your audience in humour if you can *leave out* some of the key lines. Some of the funniest moments in comedy are where nothing is actually said. It's the power of the pause. It's the power of the stare. Your audience will be far more engrossed when you give them space to fill in the blanks.

One of the ways I love to do this is **to leave out the punch line!** Yes – that's right! If you set up your story so that the punch line is dead obvious to everyone, you don't need to say it!

In a sermon recently, I was describing how I was once accidentally locked in my classroom as a young schoolboy. I described how there was no-one around to unlock the door for me at the end of a school day and how nobody heard me when I called for help. I was trapped.

"I'm thinking to myself 'I might have to stay here for the night!'. But suddenly I become aware that there is something I hadn't counted on (slight pause so the audience will start to be intrigued). *My bladder is filling up fast. Drip by drip – it feels like it is about to burst!* (slapstick humour). *I just have to go! But there is nowhere I can go! I am trapped in my classroom. What can I do?"* (Pause)

"Suddenly, I've got a brilliant idea. (Pause). *Our classroom has a goldfish… "* (STOP! There is no need to say anymore! Everyone has worked out the punch line already. The fact that they have worked it out for themselves makes it funnier!)

On another occasion, I was telling the following story in a message to youth pastors. I was getting them on board with the concept *sometimes you will make dumb decisions that might possibly get you sacked*. I described to them what happened at the youth group where I became a Christian:

"We have a large youth group with a whole stack of kids from the local community. Picture this: tonight, a few of the 16-year-old boys are thinking it would be real fun to sneak in one of those tiny bottles of incredibly potent alcohol and quietly get drunk as the youth group night progresses.

"Our youth pastor spots this before anything can happen, and he confronts the boys. He is making a deal with them. 'Go and empty the bottle; bring back the empty bottle; then I'll smell your breath to make sure you haven't drunk it yourself; and if you bring me back the empty bottle, I'll say no more about this on the condition that you never do anything so silly again.' So

the boys go out and empty the bottle, they bring it back and the night proceeds without any further incident.

"What our youth pastor doesn't realise is... when they are looking for somewhere to empty the bottle, as they are walking through the church kitchen... (slight pause, as the audience is starting to anticipate that something is about to go wrong) *...they notice some half-empty bottles of cordial."* (STOP! No need to fill in the details. Everyone has already worked it out!)

After the laughter has subsided, there is a surprise punch line where again you don't need to spell out the details. *"On Sunday morning at Sunday School..."* (STOP! That's all you need! The story finishes there. The audience gets more fun when they can work out the punch line themselves.)

Sometimes the funniest line is when you say nothing at all.

i. Tailor your humour for the culture of your audience

Different audiences will laugh at different things. And every national background will produce its own favourite brand of laughter. You don't have to know all these fine nuances – but if you're speaking outside your own culture, road-test a few of your stories to make sure they will work. Also be aware of stories that include reference to high levels of wealth and technology if you are speaking in a more developing region of the world.

Different ages will enjoy different styles of humour – and will make fun of different sorts of people. Over the page is a quick guide to a few different age groups.

This list is not meant to be exhaustive, but will give you a quick overview. Remember, if you're speaking to an age group that you're not familiar with, road-test some of your stories first. You can even use extended family members to help with this.

Age group	Preferred humour
Children	Lots of stories; lots of action; lots of slapstick
Junior High	Pants falling down; pie in the face; toilet jokes; slapstick; jokes about parents
Senior High / Young adult	Starting to enjoy witty, clever humour. They love stories about boy/girl romances. Jokes about parents and teachers. They are starting out in the adult world – talk about their immediate future. Funny stories about how older people don't tolerate them
Young marrieds	Wedding jokes; stories about babies and childbirth
Parents of teens	Stories about coping with teens; the dopey things that teens do. They are beginning to enjoy stories about getting older and the hassles that brings
Older folk	Love remembering the way the world used to be. They love to gently make polite fun of the fashions, fads and follies of young people ("Born with surgically implanted earphones")

However funny you think you are, or aren't, if you follow these principles, you will sharpen your humour to be an effective agent in helping you to take your passengers to the chosen destination.

Chapter 23

Nine humour techniques that really work

O f all the humour techniques that exist, here are my absolute favourites. Remember, the key element of humour is surprise.

1. Anti-climax

This is similar to the crescendo I mentioned in Chapter 19. The humour (and the surprise) in anti-climax is that you set up the audience to expect that the final moment in your list will hit the dizzy heights. But in fact your final item is quite dull and mundane (and perhaps embarrassing):

He went on to conquer his fears.
He went on to conquer his world.
Too bad he couldn't conquer his acne.

Remember the element of surprise. Set your audience up with an expectation – and then surprise them with an anti-climax.

2. Stating the obvious

This is where you set up the audience to expect a surprise, but you tell them something which was already blindingly obvious.

One of our high-school students was preaching at his school chapel service. He is Korean born, but was adopted as a baby and brought up in Australia by western parents. So he is a very Aussie kid, but he looks incredibly Asian.

Here's how he started his talk at school. Notice how his stating the obvious catches his audience by surprise:

"I have a confession to make. I've never really come right out and said this. Some of you have kinda worked it out, but today I'm coming clean. Today I'm coming out. Here it is: (pause) 'I... (pause) am... (longer pause) Asian!'"

He stated something which was patently obvious. That was the surprise. The whole chapel erupted with laughter.

3. Understatement

You can often achieve humour by intentionally understating a volatile situation. Understatement often works well when it immediately follows an exaggeration.

There was a rock-climber high up on a cliff. The tiny ledge where he was resting his feet was starting to crumble. And at the last moment, as his feet gave way, he reached out with his hand a grabbed onto a small bush just above him. There he was. Hundreds of feet up a cliff. His whole life hanging before him. Above him was an impassable outcrop. Below him was sudden death.

He was in what the philosophers like to call an "existential predicament".

Understatement. It catches the audience by surprise and produces a humorous effect.

4. Absurdity

There are so many situations in life that are absolutely absurd. They don't look absurd because we've grown used to them. The way to surprise your audience is to describe to them something that they have always accepted as commonplace, and yet, by your skilful words, you surprise them by showing them the absurdity of it all. You help them to see that life is different from what they thought it was.

I was describing in a message how our lives are ruled by fear. I had recently erected a basketball ring in our backyard for our son, and I was intrigued by the safety precautions that came with the instruction manual. (The quotes below are really from the manual!). Here are my notes:

Recently I assembled one of those basketball contraptions in our backyard – as a Christmas present for my son Josh. Everything was going fine until I read the warnings on the instruction leaflet. (This has now created interest in my listeners – they are starting to wonder what it might say).

I quote: 'To ensure your safety, do not attempt to assemble the ProCourt System without following the instructions carefully … if you ignore any of these instructions, it could cause serious personal injuries such as cuts (pause), *broken bones* (pause), *nerve damage (pause and look up), spinal injury* (pause and grimace), *brain injury or* (long pause) *death.'*

If I get one thing wrong, my son could die. They didn't say that in the ad. "Buy the ProCourt Basketball system, and enjoy endless hours of summer fun, or (pause) *sudden death". I didn't realise the fatal power of this toy until I opened the 14-page instruction book. That basketball contraption stands there in our back yard like a gallows. Whenever Josh says "I'm going out to play basketball" I feel like saying: "Well, I want you to know that I've always loved you…"*

There's no need to add more. That is the punch line. The audience can work out the rest for themselves.

Absurdity. So many things in life are ridiculous. Show us how ridiculous they are, and we will laugh. And if something isn't ridiculous in its normal form – then exaggerate it a little to show us how absurd it really is.

5. The cynical truism

This is where you describe a situation that everyone knows about, and that everyone resents. Prime targets of this will always be government programmes that flop; traffic jams; public transport; or politicians' promises that will never see the light of day.

I was telling a story about how I was made the goalkeeper in my under-12 soccer team. I was trying to convey to the audience how special the role of the goalkeeper was. I wanted to alert them to one of the special privileges – that in the team photo it is the goalkeeper who gets to hold the soccer ball (which is in itself an anti-climax).

Here's how I said it, using a cynical truism to raise a laugh:

> *"There are so many special privileges in being a goalkeeper. Guess who gets to hold the soccer ball in the annual team photo? It's not the captain… it's not the coach's son…* (dropping of voice) *… although they're usually the same person…* (raising of eyebrows).*"*

We all know that the coach's son often ends up being the captain. And deep down we resent that. So to highlight it – bring out the innate humour of it.

6. The surprise punch line

This is where you tell a story which is funny – and the audience thinks it is over – and then you surprise them with an extra punch line at the end.

I was speaking at our junior-high youth group, and I wanted to tell them a story about starting to do something without checking that everything is ready. *(If you wonder why I am telling a toilet story to junior-highs, then read my section on "age-appropriate humour")*

I told them the story about how I was doing some individual training at the soccer fields, and I needed to use the toilet. I described how the place was deserted except for me. I let them know that I entered the cubicle, sat down, and completed the operation.

"Now that the operation was complete, there was only the (clear throat, look embarrassed) *paperwork to be done. And then I realised that there was something I should have checked before I had commenced the whole operation. I looked over at the toilet roll holder and...* (pause for a moment and let them fill in the blanks. Laughter is now starting to slip out)... *THERE WAS NO TOILET PAPER!* (They think this is the punch-line. But wait – there's more!)

What was I to do? I couldn't call for help – there was nobody else there. I couldn't just finish without the final paperwork – it would have been way too messy. I was absolutely stuck on that toilet.

"And then I noticed something on the floor just outside the cubicle. It was the weekly soccer-club newsletter. (No need to say anymore – they can work it out for themselves. They are screaming with laughter at the thought of my using the soccer newsletter as toilet paper).

"So remember – before you start to do anything – check that you've got everything ready first." (They think that is the end of the story ... but the surprise punch-line is about to come). *Maybe next time I should take the staples out?"* (Howls of laughter. The extra punch-line caught them absolutely by surprise.)

7. Slapstick

Used sparingly, slapstick – *or visual humour* – can be very effective. Especially with young people!

I was telling a story at my youth group about how I did stupid things when I was at school. I told them about a time when I was in my first year of school as a five-year-old. There was a girl I liked, and I was trying to work out a way to let her know I liked her.

> *"It was lunchtime. Everyone was sitting around the schoolyard eating their lunch. I said to myself "Tim – it's now or never! You have to let her know that you like her". So I went over and stood very close to her – and then I made my move ...* (slight pause to cause the audience to wonder "what did he do?") ... *I SAT DOWN IN HER LAP!* (laughter – they think this is the punch-line)
>
> *"There was one thing I didn't realise* (pause – to intrigue people). *For lunch that day – she was eating a meat pie.* (pause for more laughter). *That meat pie was in her lap. So when I sat down in her lap, I sat right down in the middle of her meat pie. When I stood up, I had bits of meat, and pastry and gravy dripping off my little blue shorts. All the other kids laughed at me and called me 'pie-pants'."*

Where's the slapstick? The whole routine is slapstick. It's a visual gag from beginning to end. I act out everything as I say it. Sitting in her lap – running around with gravy dripping off my shorts. Slapstick. An oldie and a goodie.

8. Sight gag

Every now and again, you can use a prop to produce humour. Again, the source of the humour is the surprise of the prop.

I was preaching at church shortly after our worship band had produced its first CD. Some of our musos were complaining that they didn't get to play on the CD. So I picked up on this complaint, and started whining that I hadn't been asked to play on the CD (which in itself was funny, because I have nothing to do with our worship band!).

"I don't know why they didn't include me on the CD. I went to our musical director and I showed him my musical instrument. But he didn't seem impressed. He said "Don't call us – we'll call you". But I've brought my instrument with me tonight. Shall I take it out? Come on – you tell me what would be wrong with using this on our next CD?

I then reached for my guitar case and I pulled out... a set of bagpipes! Laughter everywhere. I couldn't actually play the bagpipes – but as a sight gag, they were worth a laugh.

9. Juxtaposition

Sometimes when two or more things are placed together, it causes humour (often accidentally). That is, neither of the things is funny within itself, but being placed right next to something which is bizarrely opposite creates the surprise – and the humour.

There are some things in life that make no sense at all. I heard about a convent – you know, a big old house where nuns live – that was having trouble with trespassers. So they had a huge sign erected at the front of their property which read like this:
*   'Trespassing absolutely prohibited. Violators will be prosecuted to the fullest extent of the law' – Signed – The Sisters of Mercy'."*

The surprise – and the humour – is in the juxtaposition of the very last word with the uncompromising warning.

There are many more humour techniques that you can learn. But these are the ones that work for me. I love them!

Chapter 24

How to move away from your notes

H ere's the dilemma for all public speakers:

- the most effective communication will occur when you are **speaking directly** to the audience without relying on notes.
- but if you don't use some notes, you easily lose your way and end up with a **less clear message!**

All speakers face this issue. All of us deal with it in different ways. At one end of the spectrum, you have note-bound, lectern-hugging speakers who read every word – word for word – and never vary anything. At the other end of the spectrum, you have free-wheeling mavericks who waltz all over the stage, but *umm* and *err* and ramble and repeat themselves, and leave key things out, and go way overtime because they don't have any notes to keep them on track.

There are far weightier tomes than this that will give you all sorts of ideas as to how to deal with this dilemma. But can I share with you what has worked for me?

1. In your early years, use full notes
If you're going to make a mistake in your early years of preaching – that is – if you might make the mistake of being too tied to your

notes, or perhaps the other mistake of going with minimal notes but forgetting half of what you're meant to say – then go with the former. **Use full notes.** Write it all out. Word for word.

2. Have your notes in front of you

I know it's funky to go *"lectern-less"* – and down the track you might end up this way – but to start with, use a stand to hold your notes, and place this stand in front of you. It's okay. Most people expect a preacher to have a lectern in front of them. Don't place it at the side, or at a bizarre angle – have it straight in front of you. If you need to look at your notes on a regular basis, then place them straight in front of you. Why? Read on!

3. Don't read your notes – SPEAK FROM your notes

Even though you have *written* your notes word for word, you don't have to *read* them word for word. The reason you have written them word for word is to have a safety net. If ever you lose your way, you can simply drop your eyes down, pick up the next sentence, and read it out word for word for a few moments until you get back on track. That's why you put your notes in front of you. You can drop your eyes down, look at your next sentence, and then look straight back at your audience – almost as if you are reading across the top of your notes as you look out onto the rows of your listeners. If you place the lectern a little to the side, you will constantly be looking to that side – and this will take you away from looking at the audience.

If you are working from a full text, then you may need to be looking at your notes at the beginning of every sentence, but make sure you look at the audience as you finish each sentence. Keep practising this, and you will find it is not that hard. Start your sentence in your notes – finish your sentence in your audience. This will save you from slavishly reading your notes word for word and so risk disengaging from your listeners. **Make it an**

unbroken rule – that in every sentence you will look at your audience at some stage. And if you get lost? Simply drop your eyes, pick up the next sentence, read from your notes until you're back on track – and then re-engage with your audience.

4. Lay out your notes so you can easily pick up the next sentence

Don't just write your words out in continuous text. Make use of all the sensible things that will make it easier for you to spot where you are as you speak. Use common sense tools such as paragraphs, space between major sections, bold typeface for important words, and numerous headings and sub-headings.

But you need a way to easily pick up your next sentence at any stage. There are two key ways to do this – but both involve the same principle: *start every sentence on a new line*. Every sentence. You **never** want to be trying to search for the beginning of a new sentence which is buried somewhere halfway across the page. If every sentence starts on a new line – and you get lost - simply drop your eyes, spot the beginning of the next sentence, and keep reading.

Here are three ways to lay out your notes. The first one will never work. But the subsequent two will always direct you to the beginning of the next sentence. These notes come from a sermon many years ago where I was working through Galatians. Don't worry too much about the *content* of these notes. Simply compare the difference when you are able to see where the next sentence starts.

Method 1: Continuous text – not recommended

We've been working through Paul's letter to the Galatians. And we've seen that there's a group of people who are trying to portray what a "real" Christian is like, but it's not reality at all. These are the Judaisers – they're trying to convince the new Christians that the "real" Christian is the person who not only trusts Jesus, but also goes through all the Jewish ceremonies as well. They're presenting a show, where to really honour Jesus – you need to be circumcised – you need to keep a weekly Sabbath – you need to prove that you are good enough by keeping every single one of God's Old Testament laws. Paul writes to the Christians in Galatia to say- "No! Christ has set you free from all that!" The reality of being Christian is not doing endless things to prove you love God. The reality of being Christian is trusting that Jesus has already done it all.

Method 2: Bullet points – much better!

- We've been working through Paul's letter to the Galatians.
- And we've seen that there's a group of people who are trying to portray what a "real" Christian is like, but it's not reality at all.
- These are the *Judaisers* – they're trying to convince the new Christians that the "real" Christian is the person who not only trusts Jesus, but also goes through all the Jewish ceremonies as well.
- They're presenting a show, where to really honour Jesus – you need to be *circumcised* – you need to keep a weekly *Sabbath* – you need to prove that you are good enough by keeping every single one of God's Old Testament laws.
- Paul writes to the Christians in Galatia to say: "No! Christ has set you free from all that!
- The reality of being Christian is not doing endless things to prove you love God.
- The reality of being Christian is trusting that Jesus has already done it all.

Notice that I have emphasised some words – making it easier for my eye to pick up key words and phrases if I lose my way. In my actual notes, I may underline parts with a pen or make notes to emphasise some parts as I work through the talk the last time before delivering it.

Method 3: The hanging indent – my favourite for many years

I love this method because it makes it so easy to pick up the first word of each new sentence.

We've been working through Paul's letter to the Galatians.

And we've seen that there's a group of people who are trying to portray what a "real" Christian is like, but it's not reality at all.

These are the *Judaisers* – they're trying to convince the new Christians that the "real" Christian is the person who not only trusts Jesus, but also goes through all the Jewish ceremonies as well.

They're presenting a show, where to really honour Jesus – you need to be *circumcised* – you need to keep a weekly *Sabbath* – you need to prove that you are good enough by keeping every single one of God's Old Testament laws.

Paul writes to the Christians in Galatia to say: "No! Christ has set you *free* from all that!

The reality of being Christian is not doing endless things to prove you love God.

The reality of being Christian is trusting that Jesus has already done it all.

5. Time yourself

In your early days of preaching, you will have no idea how long your message will last. I have a suggestion: if you're going to make a mistake with your early messages, make them too short, rather than too long.

Practise your message from beginning to end. Just as you would preach it on the day. Preferably with a trusted friend to give you feedback. But you can do it by yourself if you prefer.

Keep a stopwatch running and quickly write down the time at each of your major headings. If it's too long or too short, you can adjust it as you revise it. Remember – when you preach it in front of an audience, it will probably take longer (with added time for audience reaction). Once you have the times roughly right, make sure that your final copy has *times* written next to each of your major headings. Have a stopwatch running as you speak, and at every major heading you should have an idea as to whether you are on time, or ahead, or behind. Then you can make adjustments throughout your message, rather than fixing everything at the end.

6. Move away from your notes during your stories

Once you have established a pattern using all the guidelines above, you are ready to start the transition to being a little less dependent on your notes. The easiest way to do this? Start moving away from the lectern when you are telling one of your stories.

If you're telling your favourite story about your *grandfather at the Christmas party*, then you should not need to read this word for word. It is your story. You know it well. Move away from your notes – stand a few steps away – and come back to the lectern at the conclusion. And if you get lost during your story? Come back to your notes immediately, drop your eyes onto your next sentence, and start reading from your notes. Remember – even though you're planning to walk away from the lectern for this story, you can still write it out word for word in your notes.

7. Start to write briefer notes

Once you have practised enough with full notes, you are ready to take the plunge and start working with far briefer notes. This will probably be a series of headings and bullet points – where you will have the *gist* of what you are saying, but maybe not the whole sentence. Here's what my full text from Galatians (above) might look like under this briefer method:

Method 4: Brief bullet points – what I currently use

- Paul's letter to the Galatians / trying to convey what's real
- Judaisers / not only trust Jesus / Jewish ceremonies as well.
- Circumcised / Sabbath / every law
- Christ has freed you / not endless things to prove your love / trust Jesus has done it all

If there is a key sentence – a phrase that you absolutely must get right – then you can always write it out in full, and make it bold so your eyes can easily drop onto it.

I left it way too long to make this transition to briefer notes. I used full notes for my first 25 years of preaching. Realistically, I should have made the transition in the first five years! But now I have made the transition, I feel much more comfortable, and my messages are becoming much more free-flowing and engaging. But don't make the transition too soon. If you go to brief notes *before you are ready,* then you will ramble too much, forget where you're going, and miss out key ideas. If you go with minimal notes before you have prepared for it adequately (see next point), then your congregation will have to suffer your verbal diarrhoea.

Under the old system of full notes, I would have eight to ten full-sized pages of typed notes for a 30-minute sermon. Now I use a single sheet – turned sideways and folded into a 4-page leaflet. The advantage of the single sheet folded sideways? It fits into my Bible – and I can take my notes with me when I move away from the lectern. Or, of course, my notes are on my iPad!

8. Visualise the flow

How do you remember what to say when you are using minimal notes – or even no notes at all?

Don't memorise it! Trying to recall something from memory can be as confining as being tied to your notes. I have never done this for a whole message. I might memorise a key sentence, or a catchphrase that I will use throughout the message, but you will do yourself, and your audience, a disservice if you try to memorise the whole thing.

But you can learn to visualise the flow. Here's what I mean. You may have ten points that you want to make in a row – perhaps there are a few stories; a number of observations; a teaching point; a challenge. Whatever they are, there are ten things that you want to say in the right order. Here's how to visualise this: can you turn each one of those ten points into a memorable picture – and then connect all ten pictures in a story?

Let me show you.

In a recent sermon about *Justice*, my introduction went like this. Here are my actual notes:

INTRODUCTION
1. **Does it really work?**
   - Mobile Phone Network / M2 widening /North West Rail / Danoz
2. **Religious group**
   - Any religion / What you're promising – am I going to get it?
   - Those St. Paul's people – are they worth getting involved with?
3. **Sermon series**
   - Generous Justice / If Jesus assessed us / be something missing?
4. **The key question**
   - "Does it really work?" = "What must I do to inherit eternal life?"
   - Separates every religion / Ask the person next to you

Let's just check back through that. I want to make the following points in order:

- Opening line: *"Does it really work?"*
- Each of the following is a story in itself:

1. **Example 1:** Mobile phone network (*notoriously unreliable*)
2. **Example 2**: M2 widening (*a local freeway where the roadworks are taking for ever and causing massive traffic jams*)
3. **Example 3**: North West Rail Line (*promised for decades – will it actually happen?*)
4. **Example 4**: Danoz (*TV advertiser that sells direct*)
5. **Example 5:** Any religious group
6. **Example 6:** Our church at St. Paul's
7. **Introduce Sermon Serie**s: "Generous Justice"
8. **Key question:** Is something missing in our church life?
9. **Key question:** How do I get eternal life?
10. **Discussion in pairs**

How do I say all that without looking at my notes?

I visualise each point as a picture. I then connect each picture in an unfolding story. A memorable, improbable, crazy, unfolding story. Here is the story I stored in my head. I had the opening line already: *"Does it really work? Someone's got a great new idea, but you want to first check out: 'Will it really work'?"*

Here is my visualisation of those first ten points:
1. There's a giant mobile phone...
2. Motoring out of the city along the M2 freeway
3. It crashes into a train...
4. That is full of 10,000 carpet sweepers (the sort of thing that Danoz would sell).
5. These 10,000 carpet sweepers fly into the air and land in St. Peter's Square in Vatican City.
6. Thousands of people run out in terror and come flocking to our church.

7. But our church is absolutely packed with high-court judges in gowns and wigs (Justice!).
8. But there's a judge with no clothes on! Something's missing!
9. He turns to Jesus, throws a giant question mark up in the air and asks a key question.
10. Jesus breaks everyone up into pairs to discuss the answer.

That's it! An outrageous, bizarre, impossible story. And yet it recalled all ten points to my mind. I did not need to look at my notes for the first seven minutes of my message. Did it take long to work out this story? No. I was running behind in my preparation, so I worked out this story during the announcements earlier in the service (don't tell my senior pastor!).

That's how you visualise the flow. You can do that for your whole message, but I'm usually happy just to visualise my introduction. And maybe a key section that comes later. This gives me the freedom to walk anywhere on stage. And when I need to get back to my notes, I simply walk back to the lectern and pick up the next sentence. If I have reached a really crucial part of the message, I usually stay at the notes for a while so that I get it right. I will often preach the conclusion of my message from the lectern. But to save me from being a slave to my notes, I have started the habit of visualising the flow in key sections of my message.

To make it work, your story must be memorable. The easiest way to make it memorable is to make it bizarre, crazy, impossible – even a little gross – packed with colourful details and full of action. That is, your story has to be outrageous enough for you to recall it easily. If you just have an ordinary story about a man going to work, catching the train, walking to his office, riding the elevator, saying hello to the receptionist and sitting down at it his desk – you will never remember the detail. It is too ordinary. Too mundane. Totally forgettable.

Notice the bizarre and detailed nature of my visualisation. There is a giant mobile phone motoring along the freeway. The train is full of 10,000 carpet sweepers which go flying through the air. Our church is packed with high-court judges – complete with gowns and wigs. (*The series was on Justice*). The clue for *something missing* was a high-court judge without a stitch of clothing on. Bizarre. Outrageous. Gross. But memorable!

Start to visualise the flow of your messages. And be liberated from the slavery of being tied to your notes. Your audience will thank you!

There are many other ways you can work with notes and other methods of remembering key points, and I have described just a few things that have worked for me at various stages. But the important point of this chapter is that the impact of the message will be more striking and memorable, and your audience more engaged, if you can step away from your notes.

Why not talk to other leaders, pastors and preachers and discuss what works for them and why? This will help you find what will work best for you.

Chapter 25

How to make your message memorable

A colleague of mine recently preached at our church. It was a great sermon. Solid Bible teaching; well presented; dramatically illustrated; and three key points. My wife and I were discussing it as we drove home.

"That was a great message, wasn't it?"
"Yes, preached with such passion."
"And I loved his three points."
"Yes – they were really solid. What were they again?"
"Um, I'm not sure, I can't quite remember. I'll have to go back to my notes."

We had both taken notes. When we checked back, we remembered what his three points were. But even though we both agreed he had made three fantastic points, neither of us could remember what they were just one hour later.

If you want to have impact with your preaching, if you want to be a faithful train driver, if you want to take your passengers to the destination of gospel transformation, if you want to see lives changed – then your message has to be *memorable*. That is, your message has to be *able to be remembered*.

How do you make that happen?

1. They will remember your stories

Let's face it. People will remember your stories far more readily than they will remember your content. This is not necessarily a bad thing. People remember Jesus' stories far more easily than they do His actual teaching. People will easily recall His stories about the *the Prodigal Son, the Parable of the Sower* or *the Good Samaritan*.

But you will find that people are not so clear on the precise meaning of each of these stories. There's nothing wrong with Jesus' teaching – but I suspect we can learn from Him to make our stories both memorable and effective. That's where Jesus' explanations are so important.

Jesus' stories are memorable. Memorable in the sense that we can easily recall to mind the outline of His stories. And effective, in that He explains them powerfully.

There are large slabs of this book that are devoted to helping you tell stories that are both memorable and effective. There is no need to repeat this here. But please note – **your stories are an integral part of your teaching. They are not some tacked on after-thought.** They are not some quickly added concession to pander to the ignorance of the masses. Your stories are key to your Bible teaching because they are what people will remember. If you can make your stories sharp and engaging – and, most importantly, effective in the way they serve the central teaching, rather than a distraction – then you will go a long way to helping your Bible teaching to be memorable.

2. They will remember your catchphrases

We have already looked at the importance of repetition – and of formulating a memorable catchphrase or chiasmus. Not every message will lend itself to a memorable catchphrase, but if you can construct one – and make it punchy and pithy, and repeat it at strategic parts of your message – then your listeners will find it very easy to recall. It is worth giving a lot of time to creating, crafting and refining these phrases

Martin Luther King was the key civil rights leader in the USA in the 1960s. And a fine preacher as well. He was the master of the catchphrase. Even those who weren't yet born in the 1960s will know of his famous message: *"I have a dream"*. People might not even know the context of that message, but they will recall the catchphrase.

If you have a chance to listen to a recording of this famous message, note carefully how Dr. King uses repetition to reinforce his catchphrases. *"I have a dream"* is repeated nine times throughout the latter part of his message, but see if you can spot the other catchphrases as well.

"One hundred years later" is repeated four times. *"Now is the time"* – also four times. *"We can never be satisfied"* – six times. *"Let freedom ring"* – ten times. If you want to sharpen yourself in the art of repetition and catchphrases – then listen to almost any African-American preacher. They are the masters of it!

3. They will remember how they felt

Emotions are very powerful. Feelings remain at the surface level of our emotional memory long after the facts and the explanations have been deeply buried. You probably know how easy it is to tap into your feelings.

When I was a boy of 11, my father died. I was there when we buried him. I lived as a teenager with the aftermath. Even though that is now around fifty years ago – and the facts of the incident are a long way from my mind – my feelings stay just below the surface and are easily accessible. All I need to do is to be made aware of a current issue where a boy has lost his father and the tears come to my eyes almost instantly.

That's why your emotional engagement with your audience is so crucial. We have already spoken of this at length, but I just want to reinforce how central this is if you want your message to be remembered. If you have made an emotional connection, people will remember how they felt. This matters – not because the feelings themselves are necessarily the important bit – but because those feelings are the gateway through which people call to mind everything else you said.

4. They will remember your headings

You'll recall I started this chapter with a story about how my wife and I couldn't remember the headings that a preacher had used – only one hour after hearing them! However, here is the point I would like to make: if you *work* on your headings, you can *make* them memorable. And the more memorable your headings, the more memorable your whole message will be.

Here are two ways to make your headings punchier – and more memorable:

a. Make your headings action-centred

My natural tendency is to make my headings *information-centred*. That is, they are the sub-points of my Book. If I am presenting a slab of information, I want to break it down into major sections. And there's nothing wrong with this as a starting point.

But your audience will respond better to your headings when they are *action-centred* rather than *content-centred*. Memorable headings need to be *transformational* rather than *informational*. Your headings should reflect your Took, rather than your Book. In other words, your audience will be far more responsive to your headings when they answer the question: *What should I do?* rather than: *"What should I know?"*

In a recent presentation to business executives, I was taking a session to help them build teamwork in the immediate group that they led. There were three key areas that I wanted to focus on:

1. The importance of listening
2. The importance of encouraging
3. The importance of correcting

That was my first shot at my three headings. I thought they were okay. They all came from the same palette (see following section) and they clearly identified the three areas I wanted to focus on.

But I thought they could be improved. They all focused on abstract terms (*listening, encouraging, correcting*). And they were information-focused, rather than action-focused.

Here was my second attempt:

1. How to listen
2. How to encourage
3. How to correct

"How to" is always a good action phrase. It suggests that very practical steps will follow. I was reasonably happy with these. I could have easily left my headings this way. But I wanted to have one more shot at making them very action-focused.

My third attempt:

1. Listen carefully
2. Encourage boldly
3. Correct gently

In the end it is a matter of wisdom as to how you finalise your headings. But look back at some of the headings you have used in past presentations. Are they *information-focused?* Can you turn them around to make them more *action-focused?*

b. Choose your headings from the same palette

To make your headings more memorable, can you make them

similar to each other? So they sound like each other; they build on each other; they repeat each other – so they are remembered far more easily?

All three examples above have words chosen from the same palette. There is a similarity between them that makes them more punchy and more memorable. But often my first attempt at headings is nothing like what I finally end up with.

I was preaching on Acts 6:1-7. It was a part of a series at my church on *"Building God's kingdom"*. As I read and re-read the passage – and re-wrote it to make sure I had a handle on it – I tried to work out what the big picture was. It seemed to me that the big idea was *"How the church of God grew"*.

I then tried to work our what the sub-points would be. That is, my major headings. Here was my first attempt:

1. Don't neglect what really matters
2. Get others ministering too
3. Get people who are filled with God's Spirit

Nothing essentially wrong with these headings. They were my first attempt to break down the passage into its major sub-points. I think they reflect the text pretty well. But here is the difficulty – *there is nothing memorable about them.*

What I wanted to do was to select my three headings all from the same palette. I played around with the headings to try and bring more unity to them. I wanted to make them come from the same family. I wanted each one to build on the one that had gone before it. Here was my second attempt:

1. The right focus – God's word
2. The right strategy – God's people
3. The right people – God's spirit

I thought it was a slight improvement. But a little cumbersome. Too complex for most people to remember.

So here was my third – and final – attempt. It ain't perfect – but it's what I went with when I preached. Have a look at it. With all its imperfections, can you see how each of the headings comes from the same palette? Can you see how each builds on the previous one? Can you see how they all resemble each other? And most importantly, can you see how they are easier to remember?

3 ways to grow a church
1. Grow with God's word
2. Grow with God's people
3. Grow with God's spirit

How do you get your headings to be more memorable? How do you get them all from the same palette? Try these tips:

- Don't worry too much when you write down your original headings. Just put down the headings that you think are best – even if they are a little long and cumbersome. As you work on the message, try and make your headings accurate, rather than punchy.
- At the end of your message, put your headings all together, one after the other. Do they fit? Do they belong with each other? Do they work together? Are they memorable?
- If not, play around with them. Try something different. If they're getting long, can you simplify and shorten them? I often have five or six goes before I end up with the headings that I will ultimately use.

But how do you make them look the same?

- Can you make them all start with the same word? Or the same phrase?

- Can they all start with the same letter?
- Can they all finish the same way?
- Can they all be verbs... or nouns... or...
- If they simply don't seem to match, can you make them part of the same palette by adding an adverb or adjective?
  - *Think carefully*
  - *Pray powerfully*
  - *Act decisively*

You will be surprised how memorable your messages will become if you take this extra work to tidy up your headings. That's why I use PowerPoint or Keynote. I don't put much on my PowerPoints (remember the golden rule with PowerPoint – *less is more!*), but I *always* use PowerPoint for two reasons:
- To help the people taking notes
- To make my headings obvious – and memorable

Do you want to see lives changed by the power of God's word? Do you want to have messages with impact? Do you want to take your passengers to the destination of gospel transformation? Then take the time to make your messages memorable. Because the more that people can put into their memory – the more they can put into their life.

Chapter 26

The whole journey

The role of a train driver is a crucial one. You get to take your passengers to a God-given destination that is well worth arriving at. You get to see real life change occur. You get to take people to the destination of transformation.

I have lots of Facebook friends who are teenagers. I live a large slab of my life with high-schoolers. I get to present God's word to them week in and week out. Many of them I hardly know. I recognise their faces – I might even know their names – but for many of them I am unaware of what is really going on in their life.

Yesterday, I received a Facebook note from a 14-year-old boy at our youth group. He is a great kid. But realistically – I barely know him. I say 'hi' to him at our youth group, but probably nearly everything he knows about me he has heard when I have been preaching out the front.

This is the message he sent me (complete with original spelling and grammar!):

Tim Before i went to camp i didnt know what it was to be a christian. When i did go to camp i was blown away by how god spoke threw you. That night i new my hole life was gonna change. Tim you are the person that contributed the most to making me a christian for that I am grateful.

For any of you who are preachers or Bible teachers – you would be able to tell me your own stories just like that. And for every piece of encouragement you receive from someone who you has been helped through your teaching, there are probably another hundred who never get around to telling you the difference God made in their life through you.

What a privilege! What an unspeakable honour to take people to the very throne room of God by opening His word and challenging them to respond. Every time I stand in front of a room of people and open my Bible, I am humbled and broken to know that God still chooses to work through me with all my imperfections.

That's what it means to be a train driver. Every time you speak, you are taking people on a journey. If you stop seeing your speaking opportunity as a talk, or a message, or a sermon, and start seeing it as a journey – then half the battle has been won.

Once you are convinced that your job is to take people on a journey, you will become far more aware of what the destination is, you'll be far more focused in making sure you take them all with you, and you will look after them carefully for the entire journey.

- **At your next presentation** – *will you get your audience on your train?*
- **At your next presentation** – *will you take them to God's destination?*
- **At your next presentation** – *will you take them to a place where they've never been before?*
- **At your next presentation** - *will you preach like a train driver?*

FRUIT THAT WILL LAST

How can you design your youth ministry so that it will have lasting impact on the lives of your young people? How can you make sure that the youthwork at your church is achieving the one thing that God wants you to achieve? Step inside the heart and passion of Tim Hawkins, one of the most experienced youth pastors around today. Step inside the inner strategy of one of the most respected and fruitful youth ministries in the world.

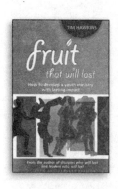

LEADERS WHO WILL LAST

What makes a good youth leader? How can you have dynamic impact? How can you lead the youth of today so that they are effective in changing their lives, transforming their schools, revolutionising their churches, and impacting the world? How can you immerse yourself in the turbulent world of young people – and keep your sanity at the same time? Come and learn from Tim Hawkins – one of the most experienced youth pastors around. He will share with you his insights and wisdom from a quarter of a century at the front-line of Christian youth leadership.

DISCIPLES WHO WILL LAST

This manual for youth leaders is packed with insights from three decades of experience. Starting from the point someone responds to the gospel, it takes you through a new Christians' first week and beyond, establishing a framework for a practical approach that brings gospel growth to young disciples.Disciples who will last aims to help youth leaders everywhere to teach and grow young Christians, so that they too will one day grow disciples for Christ.

thegoodbook COMPANY

THE CRY OF MY HEART

We live in a world where we long to be real – we long to be genuine. We want genuine relationships, genuine community and genuine success. That's the cry of our hearts – to be real in a world that is increasingly fake. This book aims to show you how to be a genuine disciple, by exploring Jesus' very own discipleship manual: The Sermon on the Mount. In it, Jesus – the Master Teacher – shows us how we can be genuine disciples and experience genuine success.

AWESOME ON THE INSIDE

'Image is everything' say the adverts – and we believe them. But God wants to do something amazing with each one of us. He wants to break through the shallowness of looks and image, and change us deep down - in our hearts. He wants us to grow to our full potential by making us 'Awesome on the Inside'. How can you grow to become the person that you were destined to be? How can you achieve your full potential? Written for teenagers of the 21st century, Tim Hawkins explores the Bible so that you can discover the big things that God wants you to do with your life.

TOTALLY TRANSFORMED

Whether you feel good about yourself or lousy about yourself, sometimes it's hard to feel excited about living as a Christian. Sure, you know it's all true, and you know deep down that you want to follow Jesus, but sometimes it's just hard work to obey him. So every now and again, you just say "stuff it", and you start living in ways that you know bring huge dishonour to the name of Jesus. If you feel like that, then the Bible has some great news for you. "If anyone is in Christ, he is a new creation; the old has gone, the new has come!"

Order from your friendly neighbourhood Good Book website:
UK & Europe: www.thegoodbook.co.uk • **North America:** www.thegoodbook.com
Australia: www.thegoodbook.com.au • **New Zealand:** www.thegoodbook.co.nz

thegoodbook
COMPANY

Opening up the Bible

At The Good Book Company, we are dedicated to helping Christians and local churches grow. We believe that God's growth process always starts with hearing clearly what He has said to us through His timeless word—the Bible.

Ever since we opened our doors in 1991, we have been striving to produce resources that honour God in the way the Bible is used. We have grown to become an international provider of user-friendly resources to the Christian community, with believers of all backgrounds and denominations using our Bible studies, books, evangelistic resources, DVD-based courses and training events.

We want to equip ordinary Christians to live for Christ day by day, and churches to grow in their knowledge of God, their love for one another, and the effectiveness of their outreach.

Call us for a discussion of your needs or visit one of our local websites for more information on the resources and services we provide.

UK & Europe: www.thegoodbook.co.uk
North America: www.thegoodbook.com
Australia: www.thegoodbook.com.au
New Zealand: www.thegoodbook.co.nz

UK & Europe: 0333 123 0880
North America: 866 244 2165
Australia: (02) 6100 4211
New Zealand (+64) 3 343 1990

www.christianityexplored.org

Our partner site is a great place for those exploring the Christian faith, with a clear explanation of the good news, powerful testimonies and answers to difficult questions.

One life. What's it all about?